BLACK HATS AND WHITE HATS

BLACK HATS *and* WHITE HATS

HEROES AND VILLAINS OF THE WEST

Harold Rabinowitz

MetroBooks

MetroBooks

An Imprint of Friedman/Fairfax Publishers

© 1996 by Michael Friedman Publishing Group, Inc.

Library of Congress Cataloging-in-Publication data available upon request.

ISBN 1-56799-377-X

Editor: Tony Burgess
Art Director: Lynne Yeamans
Designer: May Egner
Photography Editor: Kathryn Culley
Photography Researcher: Deborah Herschkowitz

Color separations by Ocean Graphic International Company Ltd.
Printed in the United Kingdom by Butler & Tanner Ltd.

For bulk purchases and special sales, please contact:
Friedman/Fairfax Publishers
Attention: Sales Department
15 West 26th Street
New York, NY 10010
212/685-6610   FAX 212/685-1307

Visit the Friedman/Fairfax website:
http://www.webcom.com/friedman

DEDICATION

To "Sir" Murray Kunkes, who, it turns out,
was conducting a grand experiment after all.

ACKNOWLEDGMENTS

The author wishes to thank the many individuals who worked, directly and indirectly, on this book, including Tony Burgess, my patient and long-suffering, but sensitive and insightful editor; May Egner, the designer of this book; and Kathryn Culley, photo editor. They have devoted their considerable talents and dedication to the creation of a book we may all be proud of. In the tradition of all of the very capable professionals at Michael Friedman Publishing, their determination to produce the best book possible resulted in a better platform, I fear, than my poor words deserve.

Four individuals influenced the point of view of this book, though I am certain there are many points on which they would disagree (not only with me, but also with each other). Howard Lamar, the dean of all historians of the American West, has educated and influenced a generation (at least) of historians and authors, and no worthwhile book on the West can fail to take notice of Prof. Lamar's work. Joining him at the summit of the mountain is Robert Utley, a scholar of incomparable standards and a writer of extraordinary skill. Forcing us to look with new sensitivities at subjects well covered by earlier authors, all formidable in the field, required a special kind of courage, and to pull it off required a special level of talent—these are Prof. Utley's in abundance. My slight association with these two gentlemen (and my intense association with their work) has inspired and sustained my fascination with the subject of the American West.

Of a more personal and direct influence have been Dale Walker, a writer of incomparable imagination and talent (and probably the best kept secret of modern Western literature), who has one of the clearest views of the foggy and murky outlines of the Old West; and Murray Kunkes, a teacher of rare ability who managed to instill in all of his students a vigorous respect for scholarship while at the same time nurturing a healthy suspicion for received views. It is to "Sir" Murray that this volume is dedicated.

Naturally, there will be statements and judgements in this book with which some or all of the people mentioned here will disagree (in some instances because they are just plain wrong). Though the responsibility for these brash statements is the author's alone, the four teacher-scholars acknowledged above have only themselves to blame for their encouragement and inspiration.

Riverdale, N.Y.

June 1996

CONTENTS

Introduction

The American government made an attempt to negotiate with the Indians, but, more often than not, valuable land was exchanged for trinkets or whiskey. The dissemination of the idea that negotiations for Indian land had been "fair and square" was the first step in the mythologizing of the Old West.

"In writing about the West, historians have also been writing about themselves."

— *Gerald D. Nash, in* Creating the West

THE HOLD THE OLD WEST HAS ON US

Probably no period of American history has left a greater legacy of heroes, villains, and odd characters than the Old West. Fascination with the goings-on west of the Mississippi River during the nineteenth century seems to be inexhaustible—and, indeed, there is no less a fascination with the Old West in every other corner of the world than there is in America. Historians have analyzed and reanalyzed the period

and the people and have created a cottage industry (hell, it's more like a whole mansion) out of improving or revising our appreciation of an event or personality of the time. The fact that biographies of nearly every important figure (and not a few minor ones) already exist has never deterred anyone from writing yet another, without even bothering to claim it to be a definitive biography. After Stanley Vestal's rich biography of Sitting Bull, for example, one might have thought another one unnecessary, yet Robert Utley's recent *The Lance and the Shield* is as fresh a biography as one would want.

And do these authors realize how lucky they are? When a historian of the Old West writes about Billy the Kid, for example, almost none of the prospective readers need to be taken by the hand and introduced to the period, the setting, or even the individual himself. The character of Billy the Kid has appeared in more than a hundred western novels, scores of songs sung by everyone from Roy Acuff to Billy Joel, and in a dozen television programs. And he has been played by actors ranging from Roy Rogers to Clu Gulager to Emilio Estevez in more than thirty motion pictures. Write a book about Billy the Kid and you are dealing with a familiar character; the very familiarity and its attendant misinformation will pose challenges, but no one is going to convince me that you will not be the envy of every other biographer.

Once, not so long ago, it was expected that we would grow out of this preoccupation and leave the West behind, remembering it fondly as a part of a national American adolescence.

But this didn't happen. To everyone's surprise, interest in the Old West has increased and become a virtual mania. The fascination with western characters and events is as great as it ever was, perhaps greater, now that they are given depth and dimension by the new wave of novelists, filmmakers, and historians. Part of the interest has to do with the discovery of the real Old West—the realization that even serious works of history were colored by a romanticized view of the people and events, particularly as they relate to the treatment and history of Native Americans. Characters that were once deemed heroic are now sometimes viewed as deeply flawed, while villains are suddenly found to have had sympathetic qualities. And now we know that much more was going on behind the scenes than the simplistic morality plays that once passed for history and the entertaining portrayals of the period would have us believe.

This means, to put it simply, that everything we know about the American West has to be reexamined. But what fuels this intense involvement with the West? Why does public and scholarly interest invite the continuing close scrutiny for this period as for no other? One historian who took a look at his (and our) involvement with the West after a lifetime of analyzing its history was the late Robert Athearn. In *The Mythic West*, published posthumously in 1986, Athearn distinguished between the real West of the historian and the mythic West of popular culture. Both are real and both have substance, and we accept both without contradiction, just as we incorporate religious beliefs and scientific facts without being numbed into confusion.

The West captures our interest and imagination in a way that other periods fail to do. We who read and think about the West, be it the real or the mythic one, are confronting something in ourselves. The myths and legends of the West lend themselves to this kind of introspection and self-exploration. And this is one reason that our fascination is not a fashion of the moment, but is likely to continue as long as the search for self-understanding continues.

The towns that sprang up throughout the West in the late 1800s were hubs of economic activity, as nearly everything homesteaders needed could be purchased only in town. Below, Deadwood, South Dakota, on a bustling, busy afternoon in 1876.

This Currier and Ives print, Frontiersmen Defend Themselves Against Ambushing Indians, *is typical of the images through which people back east learned of the dangers and challenges of life on the frontier.*

If one needed any further indication of this unique quality of the Old West to serve as the landscape for exploring ourselves, one has only to look about at how fashions are influenced by the Old West. Consider that people all over the country wear clothing influenced by western style and garb—but when was the last time you saw anyone dress in colonial garb, or Victorian dress, or even the styles of the 1920s or 1930s? Something more than simply an evocation of a period is happening here: the Old West has become a means of looking back at ourselves—at both our personal interior lives and into our lives as a society.

Robert Athearn was among the first to notice this deep connection and look for an explanation. He believed that the issues that faced the people of the Old West bore a striking resemblance to the major issues of today. Athearn identified three such areas: the confrontation with magnificent and formidable, even overwhelming, natural wonders; the confrontation with a wholly different culture with which the settlers believed they could not coexist; and the confrontation with a society held together by the thinnest tissue of law and established convention.

Clearly, contemporary society shares these concerns, and so we look at the myths of the Old West as archetypes of ways in which these issues might be addressed. Is Billy the Kid a hero or a villain? What do we, or what should we, feel about Davy Crockett, Geronimo, Calamity Jane, or Judge Roy Bean? Our highly individual responses will depend, on the one hand, on how we perceive these people confronting such serious issues and how, on the other, we hope or aspire to confront their modern-day versions.

No other period affords us this prismatic view into ourselves. Many characters of the Old West are described as "Robin Hood–like figures," but people don't identify with the legendary figure of British medieval life on a personal level the way they do with his western counterparts. In the Old West, there were so many varieties of Robin Hood figures that we can take our pick and identify with the one that matches our style perfectly. The people of the frontier embody values that we would be proud or ashamed to admit we hold dear, and that is exactly what makes them so interesting and us so empathetic.

HOW THE WEST WAS DIFFERENT

The word "frontier" described various places throughout history, but the frontier of the Old West was different from other areas to which the word was applied. The eastern seaboard of America was a frontier to the first colonists from Europe; once that area was settled and the institutions of civilization were in place, the next westward area was designated the frontier—first the inland areas, then the trans-Appalachian wilderness, then the midwestern plains, then the trans-Mississippi areas, and finally, the West. Unlike the previous frontiers, however, the West did not stop being a frontier once the first rush of settlement passed through. The special characteristics of the area were so new to the settlers that the frontier quality did not subside—for some people, it persists right through to the present day.

Again, Robert Athearn provides an explanation. The West was different physiographically. Nothing the Europeans had encountered in the eastern part of the continent prepared them for the wide expanses, the deserts and mountains, and the dense forests and vast wilderness of the West. The natural challenge was never overcome, and in this sense, the West was never tamed. In virtually every legend of the West, nature is a force that must be reckoned with. Even today, society strives to confront nature and reach a compromise that will allow us to tame nature and her resources without destroying the planet. But despite our efforts to control it, nature is still a potentially devastating force. We can empathize with the struggles of our western heroes and villains against nature, as well as against society.

Of course, the first European settlers on the American continent were faced with the fact that the land was already inhabited by another race of people. But these early settlers had different attitudes from the later western pioneers, and they dealt with the issue in different ways. Although the earliest settlers (and even some of the later ones) might have deluded themselves and the Native Americans into thinking that innocence lay at the heart of their intentions—that they were seeking only refuge, or that they were hoping to convert the Indians into Christians, or that the displacement of the Indians had been an "accident"—all such pretense was cast aside when the move westward began. Virtually from the day Lewis and Clark set out along the Missouri, the objective was clear: Europeans wanted the land then inhabited by some five hundred Native American nations, with an estimated total population of three million. These settlers were intent on establishing a nation that would stretch from ocean to ocean, and they wanted the Native Americans off the land by any means. The doctrine of Manifest Destiny was in every American's mind from the very beginning of the nineteenth century—only details of strategy and how ruthless a method should be used were discussed and debated.

In the Old West, the issue of the Indian was ever-present; it never passed out of the front line of concern as it had in the East, not even after the eventual outcome of the struggle was clear. The Old West dealt with Native Americans as the "other" throughout the nineteenth century and then thought of Mexican bandit gangs in

The reports brought back by Lewis and Clark on the Mandan Indians of South Dakota supported President Jefferson's conciliatory policy toward the Indians. The Mandans were peaceful, highly spiritual, sensitive to the cycles of nature, and friendly to the early explorers who visited them.

those same terms as the century drew to a close. But the major issues for westerners revolved around how to use their new power in a land usurped from its native inhabitants and how to establish a civilization in the midst of a foreign culture. At the end of the twentieth century, the United States is struggling with issues that aren't so different. Compared with the halcyon days of the post–World War II decades, can there be any doubt that the 1990s have more in common with the Old West than they do with the America of the 1950s?

The image of the Old West as a largely lawless, anything-goes culture is not supported by the facts—most settlers were, in fact, law-abiding and God-fearing. But it certainly was a culture that shook loose from the bonds of convention. It had been centuries since Europeans could indulge in the freedom of an unstructured society with only the most modest controls of law enforcement and social convention. Although most behaved themselves, the mere opportunity to run wild promoted a kind of freethinking atmosphere that brought many individuals into their own. Schemes, enterprises, exploits, and philosophies that would have been crushed under the weight of social approbation suddenly had a chance to flourish and either prove their worth or go down into the dustbin of history. This was not true of colonial America, or even of the Plains pioneers—in both cases, settlers brought with them a strong resolve that their faith was one of the

things that was going to protect them. Many of those communities tended to be very conservative for just this reason: awareness of the godless wilderness just beyond the stockade made the settlers cling all the more to their beliefs, traditions, and mores.

The Old West resented the restrictiveness of government and bureaucracies of any kind. It promoted a ruggedness and an independent self-reliance that extolled the individual and mistrusted organizations. It resented control of behavior by the imposition of restrictions, yet it held strongly to a code of honor in which personal debt and obligation were paramount. The unbridled spirit of the Old West was a characteristic that persisted well beyond the period of its frontierdom—again, it is distinctive in the region right up to the present day.

The populist foundation of American law—"of the people, for the people, and by the people"—is sometimes perceived to be at odds with the principles of law and order on which a society depends for the peaceful conduct of life and commerce. On the one hand, an elevated position is given to the natural moral lights of the individual who is, in the Jeffersonian view, seen as the basis of government authority through the democratic process. On the other hand, the right and need for government to enforce its laws and decisions over the claims of the individual is an overriding practical necessity. When, as is apt to happen even in well-developed societies, the powers that

The opening of the Great Northwest is celebrated in this mural, which is found in the Oregon state capitol in Salem. Lewis and Clark are at the Columbia River, near Celilo Falls; Sacajawea looks on at right.

be become corrupted by the influences of nondemocratic interests, the rights of the individual become extolled in American society as nowhere else—and nowhere more so than in the Southwest, heir to both the tradition of the Civil War and the barely civilized frontier.

One other factor makes the Old West an important period to the modern psyche: it is the last time in American history there were not too many of us to keep track of. As the populations of eastern cities grew in predictable ways, the West maintained a roominess that permitted it to acknowledge

period when a person of dubious value to society and of questionable worth to one's fellow human being can still be valued and cherished seems like a dream one dares not hope for.

OUR PLAN

In the pages that follow, we will look at some legendary characters and examine the elements of their stories that have touched us and struck responsive (or revulsive) chords. We call this collection *Black Hats and White Hats* after the old Hollywood axiom about how to tell the "good guys" from the "bad guys"—the good guys always wore white hats and the bad guys always wore black. In looking at the white-hatted heroes and the black-hatted villains—and at people who wore other kinds of headgear—we are apt to find that the distinction begins to blur as we look closer at the life behind the legend as it has been portrayed in popular story and song. It is not always clear exactly what color hat some figures are wearing—and perhaps that is just as it should be. After all, why should the legendary figures of the mythic West be any more fathomable than our own selves?

In less than a century, the entire West was populated by white settlers, while the Native Americans who inhabited nearly every corner became little more than a memory. The singing cowboy stars Dale Evans and Roy Rogers, shown here in 1992, knew only a West of ranches, rodeos, and boom towns. The original inhabitants were only ghosts on the prairie.

the place of the individual in the development of a region. The jumble that history became in the East as the population swelled, and that marked the history of each successive layer of westward expansion, is not duplicated in the Old West throughout a century of living, working, and growing. Individual acts by singular personalities mark the march of time at the end of the century as it did in the beginning. To a society that watches helplessly as every shred of individuality is crushed into oblivion by the sheer weight of teeming populations and crowded urban centers, a

We will look at a number of individuals who have been placed in one of several categories—villains, heroes, soldiers, Indians, and women. That some of these classifications are arbitrary should be obvious; most of the characters that remain in the forefront of our consciousness about the Old West were complex people, more complex, certainly, than could be captured by any stereotype. We will try to take a closer look at the real person and see how he or she might or might not fit into the category. Our interest is in seeing exactly who is under the particular kind of hat that popular imagination has placed atop his or her head. But we will also be interested in how that person has come to be perceived through the ages in books and on the screen. We will compare the mythic image to the real one, if there is something substantial to compare, and we will make note of the fact when there isn't—and sometimes we will wonder aloud how the individual has escaped our culture's attention after leading so colorful and interesting a life.

We will not—cannot—be exhaustive; for that there are some wonderful surveys, reference works, and biographies to which the reader may refer (see the Bibliography on page 190). Consider this an introductory passageway into the period of the American West, a selection of characters that has captured this author's admittedly peculiar tastes and interests. These, in short, are the people and events that have fascinated me over the years, the ones on which I have lavished the most attention when reading, editing, and writing works about the Old West. The reader might look upon this as a primer on the people of the Old West and an invitation to explore the print and film literature of the Old West.

As much attention is paid to the presentation of the Old West on film as in print; this is a testament to the changes that have taken place in our time. The cinematic art is far from reaching the level of artistic mastery of dramatic and novelistic literature, but it is nonetheless an important repository of the public consciousness about the West (as it is about many other things). It has sometimes been said that movies are a mirror of society—and this is as often considered a denigration of the art as an analysis. From this author's vantage point, it is neither; it is a statement about the collaborative nature of the art and its intensely commercial basis. Films are the answer to an age-old question: if a film is made and no one sees it, then it doesn't exist. This is evidenced by the fact that, although a play exists and may be studied in print even if

it is not performed, the time has not yet arrived when a screenplay is studied by anyone other than students of film or when a film is said to exist independently of its ever being filmed or seen.

If anything in this introduction is true, the characters chosen to investigate say as much about me as anything—but I guess that's a risk I'll just have to take.

Actor John Travolta promoting his film Urban Cowboy. *In the late twentieth century, only the mythic image of the West remains in the popular consciousness.*

ROBBERS ROOST,

CHAPTER ONE

BLACK HATS

The Outlaws

American historian Frederick Jackson Turner (1861–1932) was among the first writers to discuss the frontier as a force in American history. Whatever the fate of his conclusions (which go in and out of fashion), after Turner no historian could look at the American West in the same way.

The image of the western villain as the "hombre" wearing a black hat is a powerful one. It has some basis in fact because outlaws frequently acted under cover of darkness, so they needed dark clothing to escape detection. The badmen who became part of the folklore of the West were more than simply bandits, however. Of more than two hundred infamous outlaws, the ones who became larger-than-life legends were part of a drama that was popularly known as the "taming of the West."

After the Civil War, many southerners looked to the West as the place where they could escape the intrusive authority of the federal government. It was clear that the borders of the United States were ultimately going to stretch from the Atlantic to the Pacific oceans. But an undeclared struggle took place in the second half of the nineteenth century, between those Americans who looked forward to the incorporation of this region into the United States as full-fledged states of the union and those who preferred to see the West remain as a collection of semiautonomous territories. Over forty "wars" were fought throughout the West—episodes that took the form of feuds, raids, reigns of terror, or range battles. Although the "combatants" may not have had such abstract motivations, the issue in all of them was whether or not the western territories were going to provide a civilized domain in which to conduct business and establish a political structure. Would the government be allowed to "promote the general welfare," as the Constitution mandated, or were the authorities going to be relegated to the role of peacekeepers, empowered only to maintain a semblance of order?

The most radical form that this approach took was in the work of historian Frederick Jackson Turner, who saw the West as the repository of all the pent-up frustrations of eastern discontent. Later historians have come to realize that this view is overly simplistic and that there were quite a few forces and people at play on the stage of the American frontier, many of whom had well-reasoned and perhaps even legitimate cause to oppose Manifest Destiny as an insidious force. There was more to the impetus toward individualism and anti-federalism than just letting off a little steam. Even those Americans who fought for Texas' independence, or who established settlements in California, shuddered at the thought of the West becoming some sort of Yankee colony.

In the legends that were told and retold about the outlaws of the West, their lives become paradigms for the frustration felt by many settlers who did not have the ability or the temerity to challenge authority. The pursuit of the outlaws was interpreted as persecution; the violence that characterized their lives became a barometer of the anger felt by those who believed they were being forced to accept federal authority.

In spite of the psychotic and ruthless manner in which these outlaws disposed of human lives and carelessly threw away their own, Americans thought they saw a point to all the mayhem. Telling the tales of the badmen became an acceptable and legitimate way of expressing one's own anger and frustration, and ultimately gave the people who saw themselves as victims a measure of solace and satisfaction.

CLAY ALLISON

Robert A. Clay Allison was born around 1841 in Waynesboro, Tennessee, to a farm family. Most eyewitnesses who wrote about Allison described him as a soft-spoken man who became deadly only when drunk. Early in his life, Allison was thought to suffer from some form of insanity due to a head injury suffered as a child; he was discharged from the Confederate Army in 1862 for "emotional instability." After the war, he and his brothers went west to Texas and New Mexico, and it was there that he earned his reputation as a gunfighter. (The title of a 1977 biography describes Allison as a "gentleman gunfighter," a description his life makes difficult to accept.)

Allison went to work for Texas ranchers Charlie Goodnight and Oliver Loving and was probably among the original cowhands who opened the Goodnight-Loving Trail on which much of the Texas cattle bound for the East were driven on their way to the midwestern stockyards. Soon Allison was working his own ranch in New Mexico near the town of Cimarron. Although he was now a rancher, he sided with the homesteaders in their struggle against the ranchers. This was in keeping with two qualities that people came to expect of Allison: he had a strong aversion to joining any sort of organization, always choosing to be independent, and he had an eccentric but overpowering sense of justice and fairness. Frequently, Allison would apologize for some outrageous action and make restitution to the injured party. In one such incident, he attacked the offices of a Cimarron newspaper and threw its equipment into the river. Later, he publicly apologized and paid for the damages.

The first reports of Allison's violent, drunken temper begin in 1870, when he was

Clay Allison, photographed at the age of twenty-six.

said to have killed a man in a knife duel fought in an open grave. Later that year, reports from Cimarron, the city in which he had settled, had him lynching a man named Charles Kennedy and cutting off his head to display on a pole at the local saloon. The first confirmed account of Allison's murderous activities concerns the shooting of John "Chunk" Colbert. The two men had raced to a tie, which made both of them unhappy. As they were discussing the matter in the local bar, Colbert drew his gun and shot at Allison from under the table. The bullet became lodged in the table, giving Allison time to draw and shoot Colbert dead.

In the 1870s, Allison became embroiled in the controversy surrounding the so-called Santa Fe Ring, a group of New Mexican politicians (largely northerners) who controlled local politics and range policy. In 1875 local pastor Reverend John Tolby was murdered after writing letters critical of the ring to the *New York Sun*. Allison spearheaded a vigilante group and seized a Mexican, Cruz Vega, who was believed to have been involved in the murder. After extracting a confession from him, the vigilantes lynched Vega and went after another man, Manuel Cardenas, whom Vega had implicated in the murder. Allison killed Cardenas in his jail cell while the man was awaiting trial. The death of Vega brought his friend, Pancho Griego, a notorious gunfighter, to town to seek vengeance. In a well-publicized gunfight, Allison gunned Griego down.

With these three deaths, and after the murder of three black soldiers passing through town for which he was arrested but never tried, Allison became an outcast. The townspeople came to regard him as simply a demented killer, and he was forced to leave the area in 1878. He drove cattle for a while, getting into drunken brawls and shoot-outs at every stop along the way. It is reported that he stopped off at Dodge City, Kansas, on one of his cattle drives and was run out of town by Wyatt Earp.

By 1880 Allison was settled and married, living on a farm on the Washita River in Texas. His reputation as an eccentric remained alive. In one incident, he extracted the tooth of a dentist who had pulled the wrong tooth from his mouth; in another, he is reported to have ridden naked through the town and into the local saloon. The fits of temper that became his hallmark earned him the nickname "Wolf of the Washita." He died in 1887 when he fell off his wagon (reportedly in a drunken stupor) and broke his neck.

Allison is a type all too common in the Old West: an individual of questionable mental capacity who was permitted to brandish a gun and drink himself into a murderous frenzy. The authorities did not have the means to control such a person, and the only solution available was to force him (at gunpoint) to leave town. In spite of his anti-establishment sentiments and the strangeness of his actions, one would be hard pressed to find Allison portrayed any way at all in literature or the popular culture. It would seem that he exceeded the limit of sympathy that was accorded other outlaws and killers.

The Washita River is more a stream than a river along most of its length, and is nearly everywhere fordable on foot or horseback. It was here that Clay Allison lived out his last years as a dangerous drunk.

SAM BASS

One outlaw who became a sympathetic figure in the lore of the Old West was Sam Bass. Poems and ballads were written about him, and he became the model for the Robin Hood–type bandit, though he was more famous for spending the money he stole than for giving it away. It was reported that he tipped the porters and conductors on the trains he robbed and that he would sometimes pay for food he seized during a robbery. The banks and railroads built during the 1870s were viewed as a new form of Yankee exploitation of the South, so Bass was often seen as the instrument of local retribution.

Bass also became the model for the good-man-led-astray legend that became a popular image in the Old West. He was born in Indiana on July 21, 1851, a date that is noted because he died on his twenty-seventh birthday. He came under the influence of an outlaw named Joel Collins, and by 1874 Bass and Collins were robbing cattle drives and banks but with poor results due to the Southwest's depressed economy. In 1877, however, the gang hit the jackpot and robbed a Union Pacific train of sixty thousand dollars in gold. Bass spread the gold about generously, greatly enhancing his legend, but also making it easy for the Pinkerton detectives to track him. (His trademark became the twenty-dollar gold pieces from the robbery.) Soon, most of the gang was captured or killed, but Bass escaped to Texas.

In Texas his career in crime was unsuccessful; some of his exploits betray a clumsiness that became part of the Bass legend. The only part of outlawing at which Bass excelled was eluding the authorities. The several months of concerted effort made by the Texas Rangers to capture him were called the "Bass Wars" by Texans, and Bass was probably helped by many local ranchers who resented the banks and the rangers. In July 1878 he was joined by the outlaw Jim Murphy, who had supposedly broken out of jail. In truth, Murphy was let out on the condition that he insinuate himself into the Bass gang and inform the rangers about their next robbery. The betrayal by a fellow outlaw also became a staple of western legend.

The next bank job Bass planned was at Round Rock, Texas, and the rangers were there waiting for him. In the ensuing shoot-out, Bass managed to escape, but he had been shot through the stomach. The next day, the posse of Texas Rangers found him, barely clinging to life in a grove outside of town. He died the next day. It was at Round Rock that a Bass lieutenant, Seaborn

Texas bandit Sam Bass was shot dead near Round Rock on July 21, 1878. In spite of his career as an outlaw, Bass became a sympathetic figure in the lore of the Old West and the subject of many poems, ballads, and tall tales.

Barnes, became a figure of western lore. Wounded in a failed Dallas bank robbery a few weeks earlier, Barnes insisted on accompanying Bass to Round Rock (perhaps sensing that all was not right with Murphy). During the shoot-out, Barnes killed two Texas Rangers and was gunned down himself—surprised by a Texas Ranger who had been getting a haircut while the robbery was taking place—but the diversion allowed the wounded Bass to flee the scene. When Bass died the next day, the two outlaws were buried side by side in the Round Rock cemetery.

The images of Sam Bass that circulated on wanted posters and in newspapers depicted him as very young and possessed of a childlike innocence, which only furthered the notion that he was basically a good man driven to evil. He enjoyed racing

horses and sometimes used the race as a cover for staking out a bank or for the actual robbery carried out by his confederates. (The image of him continuing to ride after winning the race, loot in hand, amused the storytellers of the times.) He was reported to have a shy and respectful manner, and on several occasions he won the trust of cattlemen who turned over their herds for him to drive to market, only to have him and Collins abscond with the money.

A popular cowboy song, "The Ballad of Sam Bass," helped solidify the legend of the outlaw. It was collected in Larkin and Black's classic 1931 book, *Singing Cowboy*, and expounded upon in Wayne Gard's 1936 study of the legend. The judgment of the ballad was that Bass had been coaxed by Collins into gambling away money from a cattle drive so that he would have no choice but to turn to a life of crime. The other villain, Jim Murphy, was supposed to have been so stricken with guilt over betraying Bass that he poisoned himself.

For years after his death, the West saw the proliferation of many artifacts identified as "Bass relics," which were supposed to have been owned by the outlaw. These included a gun belt that now hangs in the Austin Library of the University of Texas and is identified as the outlaw's. Bass was also alleged to have buried stolen gold, but this is unlikely because Bass was not very good at robbing and tended to spend what little money he got as soon as he could. Still, several expeditions to find Sam Bass's lost gold have been undertaken in the twentieth century (none of them have found anything).

Sam Bass was only rarely portrayed in films, partly because his career was so short and partly because he was not terribly successful as an outlaw. In several productions of the 1940s, Bass was made out to be a member of gangs of badmen that a cowboy hero could overcome, but there

was no relationship between the screen character and the legendary figure. Bass first became an identifiable figure in the 1946 film *Badmen's Territory*, though he was played as an older, completely evil character by the portly Nestor Paiva. The only film that portrayed Bass in a sympathetic light was 1949's *Calamity Jane and Sam Bass*. This totally fictional film (the two outlaws never actually met) had a dapper Howard Duff playing Bass as a hero misunderstood by everyone—except Jane, of course.

BILLY THE KID

The man who became, far and away, the greatest legendary outlaw of the Old West was Billy the Kid. Billy became the archetype of the man branded a criminal by corrupt forces in society and thus wrongly accused. As the Old West was brought into American society, authority to represent federal policy— as well as the authority to uphold law and maintain order—was often delegated by Washington to factions who sought political and economic advantage. This corrupt atmosphere sometimes pitted equally lawless and ruthless elements against one another, and the sanction given one side by the federal government impressed few people. In the period after the Civil War, settlers from the South were discriminated against by the empowered authorities in the western territories, which only made matters worse.

The Lincoln County War was just such a conflict—between the local "authorities," who used their power for personal gain, and farmers and ranchers, who usually had

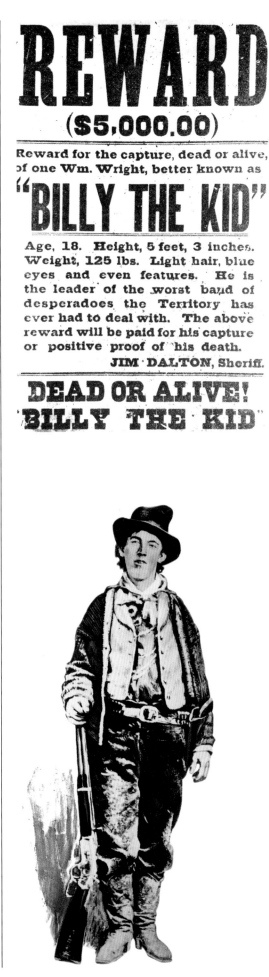

REWARD

($5,000.00)

Reward for the capture, dead or alive, of one Wm. Wright, better known as

"BILLY THE KID"

Age, 18. Height, 5 feet, 3 inches. Weight, 125 lbs. Light hair, blue eyes and even features. He is the leader of the worst band of desperadoes the Territory has ever had to deal with. The above reward will be paid for his capture or positive proof of his death.

JIM DALTON, Sheriff.

DEAD OR ALIVE!
"BILLY THE KID"

What was remembered about William Bonney— Billy the Kid—was his violent nature (opposite) and his first gun. Forgotten was the struggle that was the basis of the Lincoln County War. At left, an old tintype of Billy, probably the most reliable likeness of Bonney to survive.

no legal recourse and followed a moral code of their own. Lincoln County was a frontier area in southeastern New Mexico that was governed by a group of businessmen and politicians associated with the powerful men known as the "Santa Fe Ring" who dominated New Mexico political life. The Lincoln County group was headed by Lawrence Murphy and James J. Dolan, and they, in turn, derived their authority from Indian Agent F.C. Gogfroy, stationed at nearby Fort Stanton, and from the attorney general for New Mexico Territory, Thomas B. Catron.

This powerful group would have brushed aside any opposition had it not been for the entry into the area of two wealthy cattlemen: the cattle baron John Chisum, eager to expand his ranching activities to the Pecos River area, and John H. Tunstall, a wealthy young Englishman who moved into the area in 1877, a year after Chisum. In addition to setting up a ranch on the Rio Feliz, about thirty miles south of Lincoln, Tunstall also opened a bank and general store that directly competed with Dolan's operation just across the street. Two important local men joined opposite sides of the conflict—sheriff William Brady aligned with Murphy and Dolan; lawyer Alexander McSween sided with Chisum and Tunstall.

There soon appeared a young man of eighteen who, in 1877, had already earned himself a reputation for being a killer and good with a gun. We believe that his name was Patrick Henry McCarty and that he had come West from New York with his mother, Catherine, in the early 1870s. His father had died (apparently along the way, possibly in a cholera epidemic then raging in Kansas). Catherine soon married William H. Antrim, and the family settled in Silver City, a mining town in the southwest corner of New Mexico. In September 1874, Catherine died, and Henry, not on good terms with his stepfather (a man who worked in the local silver mines and was subject to the deranging mercury poisoning that was an occupational hazard of silver mining), moved into a hotel and worked for his room and board.

A fight with Chinese laundrymen got the boy arrested, his first scrape with the law, although accounts of the incident indicated that the real culprit was a "Sombrero Jack," a prankster who left Henry literally holding the bag. Henry escaped jail and became a cowhand in the Camp Grant region of Arizona. It was here that the young man assumed the name Billy, telling everyone it was short for William H. Bonney, probably just using his stepfather's first name (though there is some evidence it may have been his real birth name). He soon gained a

An old woodcut depicting the shooting of Billy the Kid by Pat Garrett. According to most accounts, Billy did not have a gun drawn at the fateful moment.

reputation as a gunfighter and became known as Kid Antrim, Billy the Kid, or just "the Kid."

The first man Billy is recorded as killing was a large blacksmith named Frank Cahill who slapped the slight teenager in the face and called him a pimp when they were both drunk in a saloon. Billy was arrested, but he escaped from jail and returned to New Mexico. He joined a gang of rustlers and horse thieves (with an occasional stage holdup thrown in) led by a childhood friend, Jesse Evans. Most of the cattle the Evans gang rustled came from the stocks of John Chisum and John Tunstall. Somehow,

in January 1878, Billy wound up working for Tunstall (the very man he had been robbing), and the two men were said to have become very good friends.

At this point the rivalry between the Dolan-Murphy set and the Chisum-Tunstall-McSween group erupted into bloodshed. It began in February, when a posse sent out by Sheriff Brady to arrest Tunstall on a trumped-up horse-stealing charge captured and killed him in cold blood while Billy watched helplessly from a distant ridge. Billy rode back and told Dick Brewer, the foreman of the Tunstall ranch, what he had seen. Brewer formed a vigilante group of his own and went hunting for his boss's killers. Two of the killers were captured: Brewer wanted to take them in for trial, but they were shot while trying to escape. Billy believed that Brady was behind Tunstall's death and that the sheriff was going to form another posse to capture and kill Brewer, himself, and the group who had avenged Tunstall's death. So, with four confederates, Billy ambushed Brady and his deputy and killed them in the town square on April 1, 1878. It was said that Billy the Kid killed twenty-one men, one for each year of his life, but it was only this killing that brought the wrath of the law on him.

Three days after the ambush on Brady, Brewer and his vigilantes rode into Blazer's Mill, New Mexico, and attempted to arrest A.L. "Buckshot" Roberts, a particularly gun-savvy member of the Murphy-Dolan faction. A gunfight ensued in which both Brewer and Roberts were killed and Billy and several others were wounded. At this point, although McSween was the elder of the Tunstall group, Billy became its field commander.

The great battle of the Lincoln County War took place at the McSween compound in July 1878. The five-day siege by the

new sheriff, George Peppin, armed with a sheaf of arrest warrants and a posse of more than forty men, ended with the McSween houses being set afire and McSween being killed while making a run for it (though some accounts have him being cut down by gunfire after walking out holding a Bible to his chest). Billy and several others escaped, but Chisum had had enough and sued for peace. He promised to stop funding the battle (Billy and the others were, after all, cowhands in Chisum's employ, or so they thought) if a new governor of New Mexico Territory were appointed to replace the obviously biased Sam Axtell. President Hayes appointed Civil War hero General Lew Wallace as the new governor in hopes that he would be able to bring peace to the area.

Wallace issued a general pardon to all combatants except Billy, because of his role in the killing of Sheriff Brady, and a truce in the feud was called in February 1879. When Chisum informed Billy that he would not pay him for his services, Billy and his friends began a period of cattle rustling and robbery that made them the bane of ranchers on both sides of the Lincoln County War. It was during this period that Billy became famous as a gunfighter and had his most public romances with Celsa Gutierrez and Deluvina Maxwell.

The relative peace was broken when Billy witnessed a lawyer named Chapman being killed by members of the Murphy-Dolan group. Governor Wallace offered Billy a complete pardon if he would testify against Chapman's killers. Billy accepted the offer, and on March 21, 1879, the people of Lincoln, New Mexico, were treated to a rare sight: a posse bringing Billy the Kid and several of his cohorts in chains to the county jail. In spite of Wallace's assurances and because the Murphy-Dolan partisans were still trying to wrest political control of the area, this time from a merchant named Joseph C. Lea, it appeared that Billy was not going to be given a full pardon for the Brady ambush and that Chapman's killers were not going to stand trial. (Wallace was also too busy at the time writing a book about ancient Rome in biblical times that eventually became a best-seller: *Ben-Hur.*) In the end, however, Billy seems to have walked calmly away from the jail and ridden out of town unchallenged.

More shooting and more cattle rustling followed, by Billy and his gang, and in the spring of 1880, a man who knew Billy well, Patrick Floyd Garrett, was elected sheriff of Lincoln. Garrett was married to a sister of Celsa Gutierrez, Billy's sweetheart (in fact, he was married to one sister, then to another when the first died). And he had been a

Two film portrayals of Billy the Kid: above, Robert Taylor (at right) seems a bit old and polished for the role; right, the shooting of Billy (Johnny Mack Brown) by Pat Garrett (Wallace Beery) in King Vidor's Billy the Kid, *for many the most authentic film depiction of the story.*

gambling and drinking buddy of Billy's in Stinking Springs, a town near Fort Sumner frequented by Billy and his gang. The townspeople probably thought Garrett had the best chance of bringing Billy in; otherwise it was clearly a case of putting a fox in charge of the chicken coop. Garrett captured Billy, and the Kid was tried (under the name William H. Bonney) and convicted of the murder of Sheriff Brady; he was sentenced to be hanged on May 13, 1881. Billy escaped again, killing the two deputies guarding him, and he hid in the Stinking Springs home of Pete Maxwell, the brother of one of his girlfriends.

Garrett assembled a small posse of deputies Billy did not know and went out to recapture the Kid. He was staking out Maxwell's house when Billy arrived after nightfall. The deputies, loitering on the front porch, did not recognize Billy, nor he them, and Billy walked into the house.

Garrett had entered Maxwell's darkened bedroom, awakened Maxwell, and was asking him if he knew Billy's whereabouts when a silhouetted figure appeared in the doorway, asking Maxwell if he knew who those men on his porch were. "That's him," Maxwell told Garrett, and Garrett shot at the figure from behind the bed. Billy died instantly of a bullet in the heart without knowing who had shot him.

In the following years, legends arose that Garrett shot the wrong man or that no shooting had taken place at all and that the coffin Maxwell and Garrett buried the next day, July 15, 1881, was empty. Another story had Billy making a deal with Garrett in which Billy could disappear down in Mexico with Celsa (or with Deluvina). That theory received a boost when a man named "Brushy Bill" Roberts surfaced during the late 1940s in the town of Hico, Texas, claiming to be Billy the Kid. (He even appeared before the governor of New Mexico petitioning for a pardon.) Brushy Bill Roberts was the most vocal and publicized pretender to the name behind the legend, but over the years, there were many others who claimed to be Billy or to have seen Billy, all over the West and in Mexico.

Possibly the most telling evidence that something of a ruse occurred was the fact that just a few weeks after Billy's shooting, Pat Garrett issued a book, *The Authentic Life of Billy the Kid*. The book (still in print) purports to tell the complete story of Billy's life and the circumstances of his death. The subtitle indicates the style of the work— *The Noted Desperado of the Southwest, Whose Deeds of Daring and Blood have Made His Name a Terror in New Mexico, Arizona & Northern Mexico.* Billy had already become the subject of many stories and serializations in the *Police Gazette* and in dime novels even before his death; after the shooting, five biographies of Billy the

Kid appeared within a year, but it was the Garrett biography that ensured that the legend would endure.

The book was ghostwritten by a man named Ashmun Upson, an easterner who had become a postmaster, storekeeper, and printer-journalist in Roswell, New Mexico, and who was a friend of both Billy and Garrett. Garrett later claimed that he wrote the book to answer those who criticized him for ambushing Billy in the dark. He also might have been in a hurry to capitalize on the Billy legend before others did. Many who have read the book with an eye to conspiracy regard it as a great hoax: the book is filled with tall tales Garrett knew full well were false; it paints a sympathetic picture of Billy as a likable young man, wronged by fate and the law. He forgoes many opportunities to paint Billy as a psychopathic killer (which he arguably was), which would have justified Garrett's actions in gunning him down, and he makes no attempt to portray the scene as a shoot-out or potential gunfight. Most significantly, it has never been explained why Pete Maxwell would help Pat Garrett gun down Billy, a prospective brother-in-law.

After his death, Billy the Kid became the subject of many songs that emphasized the two sides of his personality—the violent, ruthless killer and the persecuted innocent boy. Billy became forever enshrined as the good-hearted boy hunted by demonic authorities abusing their power, in a book by Chicago journalist Walter Noble Burns, *The Saga of Billy the Kid,* a best-seller for years following its publication in 1926. Burns borrowed heavily from the Garrett book and established the image of the Kid that generations of Hollywood filmmakers have found irresistible.

Billy the Kid was portrayed in more than forty films by actors as diverse as Audie Murphy, Michael J. Pollard, Buster Crabbe,

Paul Newman, Kris Kistofferson, and Emilio Estevez. In many of these films, there is no connection whatever between the historical Billy or the Lincoln County War and what is portrayed on the screen. Such a lack of historical accuracy is hardly a surprise in the campy 1966 film, *Billy the Kid vs. Dracula,* but it also exists in films such as *Young Guns II* (1990), which takes another look at the Brushy Billy claims and departs from there into modern western fantasy. The two films that came closest to capturing the life and times of the historical Billy both had the western actor-director William S. Hart serving as a consultant. The 1941 film *Billy the Kid* starred Robert Taylor in a pedestrian treatment of the story, and the classic 1930 *Billy the Kid* was directed by King Vidor and starred Johnny Mack Brown as Billy, and Wallace Beery in a riveting performance as Pat Garrett.

The persistence of the Billy the Kid legend has confounded historians and folklorists, but that bewilderment itself stems from an insensitivity to the American ambivalence toward the role and nature of American law and governance. Billy the Kid

The Hole-in-the-Wall homestead was a place of refuge for bandits, but they still had to tend to ranch duties and cattle-raising to survive.

has become a symbol of the contrarian resistance to government excess, a symbol aided by the innocence implied by the youthful appellation "the Kid."

THE WILD BUNCH:

BUTCH CASSIDY AND THE SUNDANCE KID

The mystery that surrounds the death of Billy the Kid pales against the one that surrounds the fate of two outlaws whose criminal careers flourished around the turn of the century: Robert Leroy Parker, known as Butch Cassidy, and his partner in crime, Harry Longbaugh, known as the Sundance Kid. Their story is, on the face of it, a compelling one, and it is remarkable that it did not

Drawn By
Merritt D. Houghton

become widely known and a subject of fiction or film until George Roy Hill's 1969 film, *Butch Cassidy and the Sundance Kid*. As Billy the Kid became a symbol of the outlaw falsely accused by a corrupt government, Butch Cassidy and Sundance became symbols of the bon vivant criminals, men who had so good a time eluding the law and carrying out daring robberies with artistry and panache that the public lived vicariously through them. The belief that the pair eluded certain death in South America was one many Americans found easy to embrace.

Robert Leroy Parker was born in Beaver, Utah, on April 13, 1866, the eldest son of seven children, and grew up on a farm in nearby Circleville with his Mormon parents. He was a youthful protégé of a local rustler named Mike Cassidy; apparently young Parker admired Cassidy a great deal, because he assumed the name as an alias for the rest of his life. "Butch" became his nickname when he worked as a butcher in 1892. After a brief jail sentence for rustling, Butch Cassidy made his way to an area of Wyoming known as Hole-in-the-Wall. This was one of three remote areas in which outlaws of the period hid—the others were Robber's Roost in southeastern Utah and Brown's Hole, located where the states of Wyoming, Utah, and Colorado meet. These areas were honeycombed with canyons, caves, and ridges that made the area easy to defend and even easier to get lost in. Gangs used these areas as havens around the year 1900, and small communities of out-of-work rustlers and bandits sprang up within their protective walls.

Butch joined a gang that became known as the Wild Bunch, a loosely organized gang that numbered more than a hundred outlaws at various times between 1894 and 1901. The gang earned its name because of the members' habit of spending money

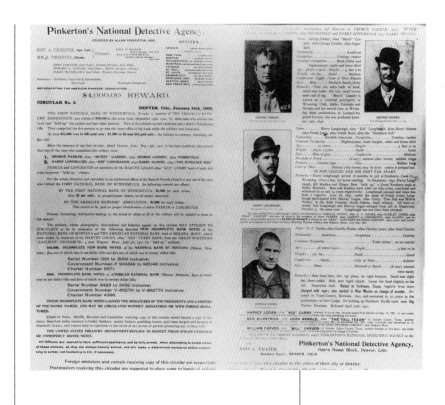

freely at brothels and saloons in Fort Worth and other frontier towns. Cassidy teamed up with a young man named Harry Longbaugh, who had a lightning-quick draw and deadly aim. Harry was already known far and wide as the Sundance Kid (a name given him when he was serving jail time in Sundance, Wyoming). Longbaugh was born either in Plainfield, New Jersey, in 1866 or in Mont Clare, Pennsylvania, in 1861. Although Cassidy was the "brains" of the duo, Longbaugh showed a flair for hiding

Allan Pinkerton was using police methods that were ahead of their time, such as (top) circulating detailed information about the Wild Bunch train robbers. Above, the gang poses for a formal portrait, which they mailed to Pinkerton. Pinkerton used the portrait on his "wanted" poster.

Allan Pinkerton, standing at right, was photographed at Antietam in 1862 as part of an espionage unit under General George McClellan. Pinkerton foiled an assassination attempt on President-elect Lincoln and then founded a detective agency in Philadelphia for the purpose of tracking down train robbers.

his identity and eluding the authorities. Between Cassidy's cunning and Sundance's draw, the pair had little trouble becoming leaders of the Wild Bunch.

The gang began robbing banks, but by this time the mining boom in the West was over and banks were no longer holding large amounts of money. Cassidy decided that the most lucrative robbery targets were the Union Pacific trains passing through Wyoming to California and the Northwest. The Reno brothers had been the first outlaws to rob trains some thirty years earlier. Their careers were short, however, as the railroads hired posses to assist local law enforcement in hunting down robbers. A Chicago detective named

Allan Pinkerton founded an agency just for this purpose, the Pinkerton Detective Agency; Pinkerton himself had been among those who hunted and captured the Renos. Since then, trains were better protected by the Pinkertons at every stop, and the safes on board the train were thicker, heavier, and nearly impossible to break open. Cassidy's response was to board the trains between stops while they were slowing down to round a bend and to blow open the safe in the baggage car with explosives. On the first robbery the Wild Bunch attempted, the blast demolished the entire baggage car and the gang spent dangerous moments collecting money that had been strewn about by the explosion.

Several robberies of Union Pacific trains had netted the gang some large hauls, which prompted the Union Pacific to engage the Pinkerton Agency in 1901, with orders to hunt Cassidy and Sundance down and bring them back dead. The relentless chase of the pair by the Pinkertons as depicted in the Hill film is faithful in many details (if not in the use of modern colloquialisms, part of the film's charm), and the pair escaped to New York City in February 1902 with their companion, Etta Place.

Place was mainly Sundance's girlfriend, though she also seems to have been romantically involved with Cassidy. (Cassidy had a sweetheart of his own, Mary Boyd, who remained loyal to him throughout his life.) Place had been born and raised in Denver, where she was a school teacher; reports of the time (and several photographs) show her to have been a beautiful woman. Her experience with schoolchildren probably helped her deal with the two overgrown youngsters leading the Wild Bunch. In New York City, the trio lived high and enjoyed the city's pleasures. They even had pictures of themselves taken in a studio and tauntingly mailed copies to the Pinkerton Agency. (Typically, the Pinkertons used these in the pair's wanted posters.)

Believing they were not going to be able to elude the Pinkertons forever, the three sailed for South America in 1902 and set up a ranch in Argentina. They were soon forced to move to Bolivia when Sundance shot a rancher who believed that the outlaw was trying to seduce his wife. The two reverted to the work they knew best, robbing banks—this time with Place participating fully, serving sometimes as a decoy and sometimes as a lookout.

In 1907 Sundance accompanied Place back to Denver, where she checked into a hospital, suffering from "acute appendicitis," according to letters written soon afterward by Cassidy. The incident is odd for several reasons: an appendix removal at that time would not have been attempted unless one were suffering from severe pain, and then a trip aboard a ship would have been extraordinarily dangerous. If Sundance and Place were concerned about the quality of medical attention she would have received in Bolivian hospitals (which were then, in fact, quite good comparatively), then Denver would not have been the closest American city to which they could go; one would expect them to first try hospitals in a coastal city. Place quickly recuperated and promptly vanished into thin air, and

The Old West was honeycombed with safe havens for bandits, where business (such as procuring firearms and fencing loot) was transacted. One such haven, Robber's Roost in southeastern Utah, was little more than a stagecoach stop.

The posse that tracked and pursued the Wild Bunch, apprehending most of the gang except for its two leaders. From left: George Hiatt, T.T. Kelliher, Joe Lefores, H. Davis, Si Funk, and Jeff Carr.

Sundance returned to South America alone. This, plus the fact that at the turn of the century "having one's appendix taken out" was sometimes used as a euphemism for having an illegitimate child, has led many to conclude that Place returned to Denver (where she had friends and family who could help her) to have Sundance's child and then continued to live there under an assumed name when Sundance returned to Bolivia.

The end of Butch Cassidy and the Sundance Kid is something of a mystery. The standard version has them robbing a train carrying a mine payroll in 1908, and taking a mule in the robbery that was known by the locals to belong to the mine's foreman. When the mule was spotted outside the restaurant where they had stopped for dinner in San Vincente, the militia was alerted, and soon a battalion of Bolivian soldiers surrounded the restaurant. Sundance was severely wounded in a hail of bullets as soon as he set foot outside, and Cassidy

was wounded as he dragged Sundance back inside. Legend has it that Cassidy put a bullet through Sundance's head to spare him the pain of being gunned down by the soldiers outside. Then Butch himself was killed when he tried to escape after nightfall through the fires around the restaurant that illuminated the night (an alternate ending to this version is that he shot himself in the head with his last round).

Another account has Butch Cassidy donning the uniform of a slain soldier after shooting his friend and sneaking through the militia lines to safety, making his way to the United States, where he successfully lived in anonymity for years afterward. In yet another story, both Butch and Sundance escape from the Bolivians and then return to the United States. In 1934 a man named William T. Phillips wrote a book (which was never published) entitled *The Bandit Invincible*, in which he claimed to be Butch Cassidy. He said he had escaped from the Bolivians, returned to the United States where he settled in Spokane, Washington, and led a respectable life. Butch's old sweetheart, Mary Boyd Rhodes (for she had married and been widowed in the intervening years) declared that she recognized Phillips as Cassidy, but Phillips claimed to have had cosmetic surgery in Paris in 1908, making any identification suspect. He died a pauper in Spangle, Washington, in 1937, wiped out in the Great Depression. A similar tale was told about the Sundance Kid: supposedly, he escaped, returned to the United States, married Etta Place, and raised their child. He is said to have died in Casper, Wyoming, in 1957. With this bunch, anything is possible.

Whether or not Butch Cassidy and the Sundance Kid died in the siege at San Vincente, this legendary pair has intrigued Americans for decades. The elements that have found the greatest resonance are very different from those found in the Billy the Kid persona. Butch and Sundance were not wrongfully accused, they were not driven by a personal loyalty, and they were not embroiled in a struggle central to the development of the American West. They were bandits, pure and simple. And although they did not wantonly kill people—their robberies were particularly lacking in bloodshed—the gang they headed contained no small number of cutthroats.

The fascination that modern Americans have with Butch Cassidy and the Sundance Kid lies partly in the enterprising way in which they went about their crime spree, approaching train robbery as a business problem to be solved with a new technique or an improved procedure. By all accounts, the pair were good-natured and well tempered; they laughed a great deal and were happy to share their plenty with others. Even if the movie *Butch Cassidy and the Sundance Kid*, which starred Paul Newman and Robert Redford, was deliberately inac-

curate in detail for the sake of comic effect, it still captured the spirit of these two men.

The central role Etta Place played in the Butch and Sundance story is also unusual in western lore. The touching possibilities of romance and devotion have struck a responsive chord in the modern psyche. And finally, the possibility that the pair (or at least one of them) cheated death and eluded the authorities is an image that appeals to the independent spirit of many Americans.

There is a cautionary note in the story of the Wild Bunch, which is given its fullest expression in the Sam Peckinpah film *The Wild Bunch*, which was released in 1969 (the same year as the Hill film). This movie is set in 1913, and the gang has evolved into a violent and brutish band of killers. Gone is the humor and pathos, replaced by the hard

The portrayals of Butch Cassidy and the Sundance Kid by Paul Newman (left) and Robert Redford, respectively, with Katherine Ross as Etta Place, were among the most engaging characterizations of the Old West in film.

steeliness of murder and gore. Throughout the film one cannot help but think that this is the inevitable legacy of Butch and Sundance. It was not Peckinpah's intention to connect his film to Hill's, but then it was probably not Butch and Sundance's intention for their train-robbing and bank-robbing ways to result in the violence portrayed in *The Wild Bunch*.

THE DALTON GANG

The Dalton Gang, which consisted mainly of three brothers—Bob, Grattan (or "Grat"), and Emmett—becomes more interesting as time passes, for two reasons: they evolved from corrupt lawmen to desperate, ruthless criminals, and they were almost comically inept as bandits. As criminals, the Daltons are portraits in failure, and their blockheaded notions about crime have still not managed to make them the least bit sympathetic.

After their father, Lewis Dalton, deserted his wife, Adeline, and the fifteen Dalton children, the family found it difficult going on the Missouri-Kansas border. The exploits of celebrated outlaws in the region, such as the James brothers and Cole Younger—a cousin on their mother's side—made both law-breaking and law enforcement attractive pursuits for young people. Sometimes, though, young people chose *both* pursuits, using the badge as a blind behind which they could engage in all manner of thievery and corruption. This seems to have been the intent of the Daltons from the very start when they went into law enforcement. Their older brother, Frank, had been a deputy marshal working for the "hanging judge," Judge Isaac Parker, and was killed by whiskey runners in 1887. The brothers then all enlisted as marshals or deputies, but it was clear that they did not feel the same way as Frank regarding the rule of law.

In 1888 Bob Dalton killed a man who was flirting with his girlfriend and claimed he shot the man because he was resisting arrest. When Oklahoma opened to settlement the next year, the Daltons did a brisk business in trading stolen horses. Soon there was no pretense, and their duties as marshals became virtually irrelevant compared with their main business—horse stealing. When they were discharged as marshals in 1890, their business went on unabated, only now they recruited the vilest collection of cutthroats and villains to be found in Oklahoma.

Eventually, Bob, Grat, and Emmett traveled to California where their brother Bill was showing promise as a politician. The three brothers engaged in several unsuccessful holdups, which resulted in their faces appearing on wanted posters all over California—amazingly, Bill did not hesitate to participate in these activities, thus ending his political career and forcing all the brothers to leave the state and return to Oklahoma. Thinking that his brothers were failures as outlaws, Bill joined a gang known as the Oklahombres, but he ultimately had no better luck than they.

Eager to make a success of themselves in the robbery business (and jealous of the notoriety of their cousins, the Youngers), the Daltons decided to attempt a robbery that would, if successful, catapult them to the forefront among outlaws: they would rob two banks at once. They also believed that this would increase their chances of escaping capture; they did not realize that robbing two banks simultaneously also increased the chances that the authorities would learn that at least one robbery was taking place. To make matters worse, they selected Coffeyville, Kansas—a town near where the Daltons had lived—as their target. They donned fake mustaches as disguises, but as they rode into town, nearly everyone on the street recognized them, and those who did not run to alert the sheriff ran home to get their guns.

Bob (right) and Grat Dalton (far right). Below: The Dalton Gang after the Coffeyville Raid on October 5, 1892, in which (from left) Bill Powers, Bob and Grat Dalton, and Dick Broadwell were killed. (Emmett was wounded.)

On October 5, 1892, the day of what came to be called the Coffeyville Raid, construction was under way in the street in front of one of the banks, so the gang dismounted and put their horses in an alleyway a block away from the banks.

The gang of five then split up: Bob and Emmett hit the First National Bank while Grat and two others hit the Condon Bank. Bob and Emmett were able to get twenty thousand dollars, but things did not go as well for Grat. While he was waiting for the

time lock to open the vault, he noticed that armed citizens were gathering outside. By the time the two teams left the banks, the townspeople had all but surrounded the banks with guns at the ready. A gunfight followed the robbers to the alleyway. The shoot-out there lasted for less than five minutes. In the end, Bob and Grat and the two other gang members (Dick Broadwell and Tim Evans) were dead, and Emmett was badly injured. Four townspeople had been killed in the raid, so Emmett was given a life sentence in 1893.

A year into Emmett's sentence, he married his childhood sweetheart, Julia Johnson, in the prison chapel. Emmett was finally pardoned in 1907, and he and Julia settled first in Tulsa, Oklahoma, and a year later in California. He became a successful real estate developer, appeared in several westerns (including one about the Coffeyville Raid called *Beyond the Law*), and wrote a book about his career in crime, *When the Daltons Rode*, which was made into the 1945 movie *The Daltons Ride Again*. He also became a staunch promoter of law and order and crusaded for prison reform until his death in 1937.

Had it not been for the debacle of the Coffeyville Raid, the Daltons might have been completely forgotten by history. It was the sheer magnitude of their failure, underscored by a grisly photograph of the dead bank robbers taken on that day, that served to immortalize the brothers and their cohorts. In a way, the Coffeyville Raid and the failed careers of the various members of the Dalton Gang marked the transition of the West from a lawless frontier to a civilized part of the United States. But still today, we sometimes find that there is a fine line between the criminal and the law enforcer. This may help to provide an explanation for the continued interest in the Dalton Gang and others of their ilk.

Above: Emmett Dalton, photographed years after the Coffeyville Raid, when he was a prosperous builder and civic leader in California. Left: An 1894 woodcut depicting the shooting of Bill Dalton at Elk in Indian Territory.

A remarkable photograph found in a New Mexico saloon, purporting to show Jesse James (left), Frank James, and their mother.

FRANK AND JESSE JAMES

Although the James Gang was active immediately after the Civil War (relatively early compared with other famous outlaws of the period), elements of their career indicated methodical minds at work and a sophisticated approach to robbing. They were the first bank and train robbers to carefully "case" the target of their robbery before striking. They took special pains to acquaint themselves with the law enforcement resources of the town or institution they were going to rob. There was a conscious attempt to deprive officials of any useful descriptions or photographs, and they made special efforts to establish alibis for the times their robberies were committed. They also managed to convince the local population that they were robbing from the wealthy railroads and banks (which they claimed had stolen the James homestead) so that they could give the money to other poor people—patently false claims. By writing letters to newspapers and conducting whisper campaigns in the towns, they were able to get the local populations to help them. Locals hid them from pursuing Pinkerton agents, gave the authorities false information on the robberies and about the outlaws' whereabouts, and some-times helped them escape by providing horses, food, and supplies. In truth, the James brothers were cut from the same cloth as the other bandits of the West—they held human life cheap—and in time the general population came to realize this and turned on them. But for a while (and in the mirror of history and legend), the James boys held a high place alongside Billy the Kid as beloved rogues.

Frank James was born in Clay County, Missouri, on January 10, 1843, to a Baptist preacher named Robert James, and his wife, Zerelda. His brother Jesse was born on September 5, 1847. In 1850 Robert James caught "gold fever" and left to seek his for-tune in California, but he soon became ill and died. Shortly after, Zerelda married a man who abused both her and the children, and after divorcing him, she married again. This time she chose a kindly man, Dr. Reuben Samuels (though it is not known exactly what sort of doctor he was), who cared for both her and her children. The family owned slaves, so the boys went to fight for the Confederacy. Frank joined the band of marauding guerrillas known as Quantrill's Raiders, and Jesse joined a simi-lar group that was led by Bloody Bill Anderson. Both brothers participated in the notorious raid and massacre conducted by Quantrill on Lawrence, Kansas. And Jesse was involved in the ambush by Anderson's band on the regiment led by Major A.V.E. Johnson that was sent to stop them.

During the war, because he was so young, Jesse was often dressed in women's clothing and sent ahead by Anderson to spy on the Union encampment. Jesse brought this experience to bear when the war was over and he turned to a life of crime. It was a natural transition for the boys; they were cousins of the notorious bandits the Younger brothers, and the war had left

Left: Jesse James at seventeen, as a Civil War guerrilla under William "Bloody Bill" Anderson. Below: Public opinion about the James boys is clear in this woodcut of Frank James being cheered by support-ers after his acquittal in Huntsville, Alabama, in 1884.

them with no other means of support. As is the case with many other criminals, they were known to be outgoing and free-spirited, and many citizens lived vicariously through them. But fundamentally they were sociopaths—perhaps even psychopaths—who would have turned to crime in virtually any circumstance. Toward the end of the war, Jesse was badly wounded and had to be nursed back to health by his cousin and lifelong sweetheart, Zerelda Mimms. They married in 1874, had two children—Jesse and Mary—and lived in the vicinity of

The James brothers—Jesse at right; Frank seated—with Fletcher Taylor during their Confederate Army days, circa 1864.

Nashville, Tennessee, an area to which the James brothers would repair when things got hot.

The first documented James Gang robbery took place on February 13, 1866, in Liberty, Missouri, and for the next nine years, they staged a series of robberies across the Plains states that made them celebrated outlaws. The gang always wore masks—the classic bandanna over the mouth and nose—so it was not certain who had done the robbing. Gunplay was frequently involved in the robberies and people were killed, but the inability of witnesses to identify the culprits kept the James boys out of jail. Their method was so well known and showed such careful planning that there was no doubt in anyone's mind that it was the James Gang's work. (In one robbery, a horse was left behind, and items found in the saddlebags were stamped "Property of Jesse James." Amazingly, James had an alibi and was not arrested.)

After a string of successful train robberies, the Pinkertons were put on the case, and now the James brothers were up against equally methodical adversaries. On January 25, 1875, acting on an erroneous tip, the Pinkertons surrounded the Samuels home and, believing Frank and Jesse to be there, lobbed gasoline bombs inside. The outlaws were not there, but their mother lost an arm and their stepbrother, Archie Samuels, was killed. The incident was widely reported and Jesse stoked the controversy by writing letters to many papers, with the end result that public opinion was clearly sympathetic to them and critical of the Pinkertons.

Then, on September 7, 1876, they made the mistake of trusting other outlaws (their cousins the Younger brothers) and attempted a joint robbery of a bank they had not staked out themselves. The Youngers may have told them that the bank in Northfield,

Minnesota, was lightly guarded, but they were unaware that the town had devised a warning system that would alert the citizenry when a robbery was in progress. When the James and Younger gangs left the bank, there was a small army of townspeople there to meet them. All the bandits were shot dead except Frank and Jesse, who somehow managed to escape.

The robbery suddenly turned public opinion against them and the brothers decided it would be best to lay low for a while. For the next three years they kept moving and refrained from robbing. They eventually settled in St. Joseph, Missouri, and Jesse adopted the name Thomas Howard. But in 1881 the James brothers had assembled a new gang and were back robbing trains and banks.

On July 15, 1881, during a robbery of the Chicago, Rock Island, and Pacific Railroad train out of Kansas City, a conductor and passenger were killed. Missouri governor Thomas Crittenden placed a ten-thousand-dollar bounty on the heads of Frank and Jesse James. Two brothers named Ford were members of the gang and had known the James brothers since their arrival in St. Joseph. Bob Ford met with Governor Crittenden and arranged for pardons, plus the reward, if he and his brother killed or captured Jesse and Frank. On the evening of April 3, 1882, Jesse had already gotten wind of the fact that the Ford brothers were preparing to betray them, and while he was arranging a picture on the wall and contemplating his next move, Bob Ford walked into the room and shot Jesse in the back of the head. Frank escaped but turned himself in a few months later.

The trials of Frank James—he was tried three times, twice in Missouri and once in Alabama—ended with his acquittal; the public sympathy for the James Gang was simply too great to allow for a successful prosecution. From the day of his release in

More than any other outlaw, Jesse James was a beloved figure of the Old West. This depiction of Jesse single-handedly fending off an attack by Pinkertons could be found in many homes in the Eastern United States.

Bob Ford poses with the gun with which he shot Jesse James. The photo was taken shortly after the shooting and was widely distributed by an enterprising photographer.

1885 to his death in 1915 at the age of seventy-two, Frank James was said to have led an honest, law-abiding life. He teamed up with Cole Younger in 1903 to stage a Wild West show that enjoyed moderate success. Frank and Jesse's mother, Zerelda Samuels, made a cottage industry of selling mementos of Jesse James, offering pebbles from his grave (which she gathered from a nearby creek) and auctioning so many guns that Jesse was reputed to have used that he would have had to have an entire arsenal.

Naturally, rumors abounded after Jesse's death that Ford had shot the wrong man and that Jesse lived in Guthrie, Oklahoma, until he died in 1948. Photographs clearly show the dead Jesse James, however, and the state of Missouri made sure of that before pardoning the Fords and paying them the five-thousand-dollar bounty (only half because they had allowed Frank to escape). Continuing doubts about whether Jesse was really the man in his grave led to an exhumation in 1995. Preliminary DNA tests proved that Jesse was, in fact, the right man, and his remains were reinterred. An honor guard in Confederate-era uniform was present at this second funeral.

Jesse James became the subject of ballads and folk tales throughout his life and even more so after his death. A number of tales illustrate the contempt he had for the law agencies pursuing him and are meant to show his sense of humor. In one story, he interrupts a preacher urging his listeners to reject the lawlessness of Jesse James to inform him and the crowd that the bank has just been robbed—as it turned out, by the James Gang. In another tale, he recognizes a Pinkerton detective he knows is after him, buys him a drink, and the Pinkerton, unaware of who his drinking buddy is, says that he wishes he could gaze upon Jesse James just once before he dies. James then sends the Pinkerton man a postcard telling him that he *has* seen Jesse James.

"The Ballad of Jesse James," one of the most popular "outlaw ballads" ever written, was the work of Billy Garshade, a Clay County resident who knew the James family. When Jesse James was shot by Bob Ford, he was living under the alias (known to everyone) of Thomas Howard, which gave rise to the most famous lines of the ballad: "That dirty little coward that shot Mr. Howard/Has laid poor Jesse in his grave."

The early books about the James-Younger gang—for many years the two groups were identified together—and the shows and lectures by Frank James and Cole Younger perpetuated the image of Jesse James as a charming rogue with a broad and generous sense of humor. They downplayed the fact that Jesse took a certain delight in simply shooting people dead (a quality that stood him in good stead when he worked for Quantrill and Anderson).

Jesse James has been portrayed in about twenty films, about half as many as Billy the Kid. These portrayals range from the ridiculous, as in the 1966 camp film *Jesse James Meets Frankenstein's Daughter*, to the wholly fictitious 1954 film *Jesse James vs. the Daltons* (actually about a meeting between Jesse James's son and the famous outlaw brothers), to the 1959 Bob Hope comedy *Alias Jesse James*, in which Hope is mistaken for the notorious outlaw. A film that has

Jesse James in his coffin in a St. Joseph, Missouri, funeral home, April 1882. The photograph was taken by A.A. Hughes, and prints were sold as souvenirs for years afterward.

The Younger brothers at the time of their 1876 trial for the Northfield Raid. From left: Cole, Jim (with a bandaged upper lip, where he was wounded during the hold-up), and Bob.

been noted for its fidelity to historical detail is the 1953 film *The Great Jesse James Raid*, about the Northfield robbery that marked the end of the James-Younger alliance. In *The Last Days of Jesse James* (1986), Johnny Cash and Kris Kristofferson play brothers only four years apart and June Carter (!) plays their mother. In several films, Jesse James appears as an incidental character, as in *Kansas Raiders*, a well-reviewed 1950 film about Quantrill's Raiders in which a young Jesse James, played by Audie Murphy, appears. In 1949 Dale Robertson received strong notices when he appeared as Jesse James in a minor role in the film *Fight Man of the Plains*.

The classic portrayal of Jesse James, however, is that of Henry Fonda in the 1939 Henry King film *Jesse James*, which portrays James as a misunderstood lad forced to rob trains by the unscrupulous railroads and banks. The image was repeated and reinforced in the classic 1940 Fritz Lang sequel, *The Return of Frank James*, again with the doleful Fonda as Jesse. In 1957 Nicholas Ray remade the 1939 film as *The True Story of Jesse James*, which only proved how important Fonda was to the role in the first place.

The James brothers typify the "Robin Hood" mystique. They promoted this romantic image—and it helped win them supporters at the time as well as a continuing cadre of forgiving admirers.

THE YOUNGER BROTHERS

The fact that the James brothers, the Daltons, and the four Younger brothers were related in some way gives credence to the view, held by some historians, that an outlaw aristocracy arose in the West and formed a dynasty stretching from Quantrill and Anderson after the Civil War to the gangsters of the 1920s. Be that as it may, the Youngers were, indeed, cousins of the James boys, a relationship they generally belittled, believing they came from better stock and were more talented outlaws than their cousins. They thought Jesse

James's toying with the authorities and his attempt to manipulate public opinion through the newspapers were amateurish and unbecoming to a proper outlaw. As if to prove their worthiness, the Youngers escalated their brazenness and their brutality after each James robbery.

The Younger brothers were born in Lee's Summit, Missouri, into a respectable family headed by Henry Washington Younger. The eldest boy, Thomas Coleman, or "Cole" for short, was born in 1844 and educated in a school whose headmaster, Stephen Elkins, later became a U.S. senator. Three of Cole's siblings—John, James, and Robert (born in 1846, 1850, and 1853, respectively)—were devoted to their older brother and followed him in his exploits during the Civil War. Their father entered the Union army, but the boys sided with the Confederacy. The Youngers had eleven other children, all of whom made respectable, law-abiding lives for themselves and spent much energy living down the infamy of their four miscreant relatives.

In October 1861 Cole and his brothers joined Quantrill's Raiders, and they later became regulars in the Confederate Army. Cole in particular distinguished himself at the battle of Lone Jack in 1862 and developed a reputation for being cunning and brave. He saved the life of a captured Union officer and prevented the execution of his old headmaster later that year. In December 1862 Cole Younger's world unraveled after he was accused of murdering a man in Kansas. He escaped, but in the process he killed a man who recognized him in a bar. In mid-1863, with nowhere to turn, Cole rejoined Quantrill, now branded a criminal by the Confederacy. Cole participated in the Quantrill massacre at Lawrence, Kansas, and then fled when the raiders disbanded. John, James, and Bob watched over their brother, at one point

killing four Union soldiers who had been sent to capture him.

Cole offered his services to Benjamin McCulloch, the commander of the Confederate forces in Texas. He was given dangerous missions; several involved espionage and undercover work, such as tracking down plantation owners who were secretly trading cotton with the Union. It was during this period that he met Myra Belle Shirley (the woman who would later become the notorious Belle Starr), and the two became lovers. In the years that followed, Cole visited Belle frequently. When she bore a child in 1867, she named her daughter Pearl Younger.

When the war ended, Cole went back to Missouri and was reunited with his brothers. The four brothers looked forward to settling down and starting a farm, but Cole was accused of committing a prewar murder and was forced to flee. He hid with the help of Frank James, who introduced him to his brother Jesse—the beginning of a fateful association, if not a friendship. Cole Younger participated in the first James Gang bank robbery in Liberty, Missouri, and, one by one, the other three brothers joined the gang until the four Youngers rode together in 1872.

The place of the Younger brothers in the James Gang varied over the next few years: sometimes the group rode united; sometimes the Youngers went off on their own. In 1875 they promoted the publication of a book, *The Guerrillas of the West; or, The Life, Character and Daring Exploits of the Younger Brothers,* by John T. Appler. It was a bestseller, containing a hodgepodge of truth, fiction, and tall tales, many calculated to show how ruthless and murderous the Younger brothers were. One story came back to haunt Cole Younger: it related how he had executed ten Union soldiers just to test the firing power of a rifle.

The three brothers (John had been killed in an 1874 shoot-out with Pinkertons in Missouri) planned a bank robbery in the town of Northfield, Minnesota, but they lacked the thoroughness of Jesse James. Their escape route was blocked by an army of rifle-bearing citizens who killed most of the gang and chased the survivors—which included Frank and Jesse James and the three injured Youngers—through the woods. As they ran, Jesse and Cole argued: Jesse wanted Cole to shoot one of his brothers dead because he was slowing them down. When Cole refused, Jesse and Frank left them and escaped, while the three wounded Youngers were captured. Although there had been some deaths in the Northfield Raid, a Minnesota law prevented execution for any criminal who admitted committing a capital crime, so the Youngers were sentenced to life in prison.

Bob Younger died of tuberculosis in prison. Jim was released in 1901 and became successful selling insurance—until he discovered that all the policies he had sold were invalid because of his criminal record. On October 19, 1902, he checked into a hotel in St. Paul, Minnesota, and put a bullet through his head. Cole Younger's life would probably have ended in some similarly tragic way had it not been for Warren C. Bronaugh, the Union soldier whose life Cole had saved when he had been captured during the Civil War. Bronaugh became a tireless champion for Younger, soliciting the aid of now-Senator Stephen Elkins, and finally obtaining a conditional pardon for Cole and Jim Younger in 1901. After Jim's suicide in 1902, Bronaugh continued to sue for a full pardon for Cole Younger, which came in 1903. After fourteen active years spent lecturing and participating in various Wild West shows and exhibitions, Cole Younger died in the town where he was born, Lee's Summit, Missouri, on February 21, 1916, at seventy-two.

The reputed brutality of the Youngers (especially as exaggerated in the Appler book) made it difficult for the public to find anything sympathetic or redeeming in the brothers. Because they didn't confine their robberies to trains and banks, they couldn't claim, as Jesse James had (falsely) claimed, that they were seeking revenge on behalf of all poor people exploited by the railroads and the banks. They lacked the panache and flair of the James brothers, and they weren't particularly clever or proficient in their thievery—a well-placed bullet was the way the Younger brothers liked to settle an argument.

In spite of Cole's later image as a criminal reformed, there was something inherently disingenuous about Cole Younger that made people believe that there was a barefaced liar lurking beneath his sinister visage. The autobiography that he released in 1903 contained several intemperate defenses of the bloodthirsty William C. Quantrill, which were not received very well by the public. And even Warren Bronaugh came across as a suspicious character—rumors abounded suggesting that he was really one of the Youngers in disguise.

Without the folklore foundation enjoyed by Billy the Kid and Jesse James, the eldest Younger was not destined to become an enduring figure of the West in his own right. However, he has been portrayed in movies twice (to speak of): first in a minor 1958 film, *Cole Younger, Gunfighter*, and then by David Carradine in the 1980 film *The Long Riders*, a movie that was more about Belle Starr's Texas than Cole Younger's West. It would appear, then, that Cole Younger didn't fit any archetype well enough to be immortalized in American legend.

JOHN WESLEY HARDIN

For the most part, the outlaws in this chapter were seen for what they really were: violent criminals with no respect for law or life. If their exploits were followed avidly by a sensation-hungry public, or even if they were admired for their cunning or adventurous spirit or for their defiance of the conventions of society and the will of business and government inter-

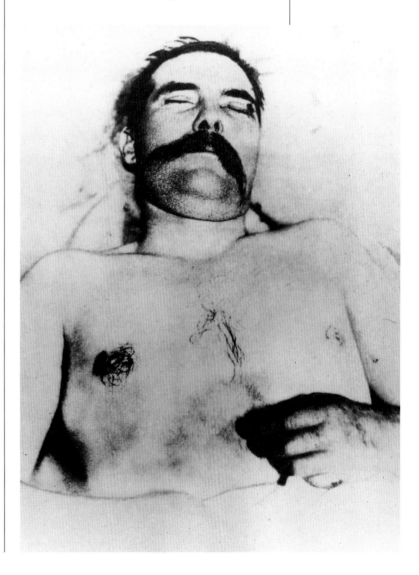

John Wesley Hardin lies dead in a coffin in 1895 after being gunned down by an El Paso sheriff.

Rock Hudson's portrayal (center, seated) of John Wesley Hardin in the 1952 film The Lawless Breed *is considered by many to be his best performance and the most vivid portrayal of a western outlaw in the movies.*

ests, the overwhelming majority of western settlers with families to feed and farms and businesses to tend breathed a sigh of relief when one of these bandits was killed or captured. The fact that in so many cases, citizen-based defensive law-enforcement groups were ultimately responsible for foiling the robberies and killing or capturing the gangs is proof enough of where, in the last analysis, the populace stood.

The well-known badmen of the West entered the domain of myth by virtue of their being interesting characters with different, often contradictory or paradoxical facets to their personalities. There were many more, however, who were simply wanton, lawless killers without any redeem-

ing qualities whatever—two such outlaws topped all others in mayhem and for this reason became legendary: John Wesley Hardin and Wild Bill Longley. Both men had violent tempers and both were virulent racists, and when they were done, they were responsible for more than seventy murders between them, many of the victims gunned down in cold blood.

John Wesley "Wes" Hardin was born in 1853 in Bonham, Texas, and his devout Methodist parents named him after the founder of their denomination. In later years, Hardin blamed his behavior on the anarchy that reigned in Texas during Reconstruction, but the truth was that he had a violent temper even as a child. He knifed a schoolmate when he was just eleven. Hardin went on to kill his first man in 1868 with the .45 caliber pistol that he was already brandishing at thirteen.

Thoroughly Unionist Texas governor E.J. Davis headed a racially integrated government and militia, and his determination to punish those who had collaborated with or supported the Confederacy created an atmosphere of vigilantism and violence throughout the state. The family of Hardin's uncle was said to have been completely wiped out, their home burned to the ground, by a band of black reconstructionists. Some historians have excused Hardin's behavior by claiming it was consistent with the temper of the times in post–Civil War Texas, but the particulars of his killings betray a man moved by pique rather than by principle or self-preservation. Hardin developed prowess with a gun and was not hesitant to use it to settle arguments or dispose of an adversary. In the decade between 1868 and 1878, he is documented as having shot dead more than twenty men.

Hardin is said to have successfully challenged the authority of Marshal Wild Bill Hickok when they met in Abilene in 1871, and he was the only man who carried a gun through the streets of the town (Hickok partisans dispute this claim, however). Two incidents solidified Hardin's reputation as a gunfighter: the killing of Charlie Webb at the height of the Sutton-Taylor Feud, one of the many postwar feuds that erupted all over the Southwest, and the shooting of deputy sheriff Charles Webb in the wild Texas town of Comanche. Webb had worked hard to convince Hardin he was friendly, and then drew on Hardin when his back was turned. The shot wounded Hardin, who turned, drew, and killed Webb with a shot to the forehead. Both killings aroused a great deal of sympathy for Hardin (mainly because both the victims had themselves been responsible for many legally sanctioned deaths that were nonetheless resented).

Webb's shooting turned Hardin into a fugitive, and he wandered through Florida and Alabama with his wife and children until he was tracked down and captured by Texas Ranger John Armstrong. Armstrong took him back to Texas, where he was tried and imprisoned in 1878. Hardin taught himself law in prison and acted as his own attorney, obtaining a pardon in 1892. His wife, Jane Bowen, had died while Hardin was in prison, and he drifted to El Paso where he sank into a deep depression. His attempt to enter politics failed, and he interspersed his occasional legal work with a robbery and a killing. Toward the end of his life, Hardin wrote an autobiography that was published posthumously in 1896. It showed insight into the violent spirit of the West of the 1890s, and it became a classic of western literature.

Hardin was eventually gunned down while standing peacefully in the Acme Saloon on the night of August 19, 1895, by a sixty-year-old El Paso lawman named John Selman. Selman had heard that Hardin had called Selman's son, the local sheriff, a son of a bitch for arresting Hardin's mistress. According to some accounts, however, Selman was primarily interested in the instant fame that would come to John Wesley Hardin's killer.

Writers and filmmakers have found very little appealing in Hardin's legend, but one 1952 film, *The Lawless Breed*, starring Rock Hudson as John Wesley Hardin, stands out because it represents one of Hudson's best performances. In the movie, Hardin is on the run in Florida with his family, and he instructs his son not to follow his example. Hardin has otherwise faded in western lore. When, in 1969, Bob Dylan released a ballad about John Wesley Hardin, most listeners responded, "Who?"

WILD BILL LONGLEY

Threw career of William Preston "Wild Bill" Longley was just as violent and lawless as that of his friend John Wesley Hardin. Longley's supporters also justified his actions by blaming the inequities and violence of Reconstruction. But the fact was that Longley killed without cause or provocation. He killed often and showed a particular inclination to kill blacks. He received his nickname after killing two black men who were dancing in the street, "arrogantly" he said, by way of an excuse. More than half of the thirty-two men he is reputed to have gunned down were blacks who had done nothing other than having the ill fortune of crossing Wild Bill's path.

Longley was born in Austin County, Texas, in 1851—to the "God-fearing" parents that all killers of the West seemed to come from—and showed his violent nature while he was still a boy. Longley often spread rumors about43

the circumstances of his killings, leading people to believe that he had acted in self-defense. This was a difficult defense for him to pursue when he was tried, for example, for killing the proprietors of a circus who refused to let him in for free.

Longley was actually hanged twice for his crimes. The first time, the hangman decided to use Longley's body for target practice and inadvertently shot the rope, allowing Longley (amazingly, not yet dead) to escape. Wild Bill Longley was finally hanged in Giddings, Texas, on October 11, 1878. He wrote a series of long letters in his last days, in which he claimed to have found religion while awaiting execution. On the gallows, he delivered an impassioned oration on the evils of crime, asserted that he was looking forward to meeting his maker with a clear conscience, and said he forgave his executioner and the lawmen who had captured him because it was just that he be punished. He then kissed the sheriff and the priest, and was hanged—almost. He was so tall that when the trap door was sprung, his feet touched the ground. The hangman laboriously pulled him up, and it took eleven minutes for Longley finally to stop gasping.

Wild Bill's exploits did not ensure him a place in history. He has been, for the most part, ignored. In a way, Hardin and Longley became symbols of the violent side of the West, indicative of the chaos that bubbled just under the surface in many areas before the settling influences of a social order and sense of community took hold.

Right: Wild Bill Longley, the man they hanged twice. Opposite: Longley being led to the gallows.

CHAPTER TWO

WHITE HATS

The Heroes

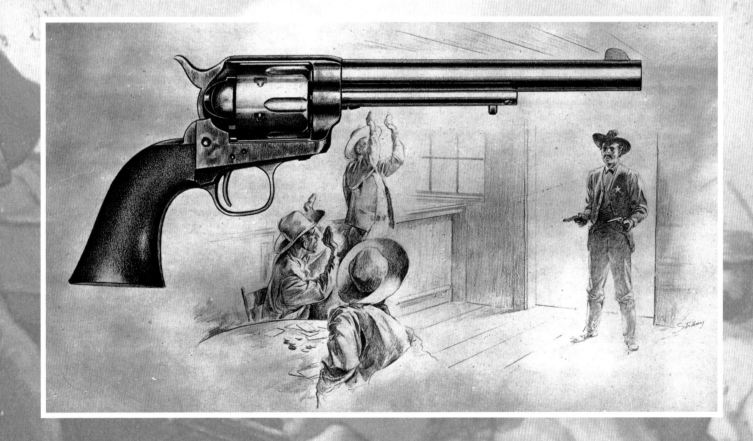

The men and women who set out to settle the West may not have been satisfied with their lives east of the Mississippi, but they were not loners and misfits. The wagon trains only functioned thanks to great cooperation among the families who joined them. This 1869 engraving by Darley and Hall shows a wagon train, led by a scout, crossing the plains.

The men and women who settled the West were faced with difficult conditions, of a kind that rarely present themselves today (although a wrong turn into the wrong place could change all that in an instant). A family heading west could, with the cracking of a wagon's axle or the collapse of an ox or mule from exhaustion, suddenly find itself stranded in the middle of a wilderness with no possibility of rescue. And often, in such circumstances, they faced certain death. Once pioneers reached their destinations, they did not breathe a sigh of relief, because they were no less prey to the forces of nature or to attacks from Indians or bandits than when they were en route. Thus, the people who did make it were survivors. They were resourceful enough to set up protection from the scourges that might destroy them once they managed to

reach their destination and create something of a home. A system of law and law enforcement was as essential to their survival as roofs over their heads and food on their tables.

Setting up the two elements of a system of law—law adjudicators (i.e., judges) and law enforcers—was no easy task. Some of the early attempts were horribly clumsy, though they indicate how desperate the settlers were to have a system of justice. The Northwest Ordinance of 1787 made provisions for the transition of wilderness into territorial status and then to statehood, with indications (somewhat vague) of how an area would go from being one of lawlessness to one governed by a civilized rule of law. But resources were as scarce for law as for everything else: judges were largely untrained and easily corruptible;

jails were usually huts or stables barely able to confine barnyard animals, let alone criminals; and officers of the law were often chosen for their ability to bully people, which frequently created more problems than it solved. A judge that applied even a semblance of rational and consistent justice (even if accompanied by eccentric behavior, as was the case with Judge Roy Bean) was welcomed as a savior from the gunplay that had previously settled arguments.

Part of the problem was that the legal structure put in place (or imposed by the federal government) consisted of layers that had inconsistent goals. The sheriff, who was usually elected by the local populace, was the first stratum of the law. He was empowered to raise posses and hold those prisoners awaiting trial, but he was also expected to collect taxes and enforce local government policy. This often put him at odds with the poorer elements of society and made him beholden to and in league with the wealthier landowners.

The next level was the federal marshal, an appointed office that was frequently given out on the basis of political patronage. Rarely was a professional lawman selected; the appointment of professional marshal Thomas Jefferson Carr as the marshal of Wyoming Territory only underscored the amateur status of other marshals. The unqualified marshals were forced to look to professionals to fill the ranks of deputy marshal, and this often became the key law-enforcement position in the frontier West. Many of the deputies (such as Wyatt Earp and Wild Bill Hickok) were appointed by local municipal governments and merely ratified by the federal marshal. A case adjudicated by the Supreme Court in 1889 involved a deputy federal marshal who killed someone he believed was attacking a state supreme court justice. The verdict set down the

In many cases erratic law, such as that administered by Isaac Parker, "the Hanging Judge," was better than no law at all.

principle that marshals and their deputies were beyond the authority of state law, making each a virtual one-man judge-jury-and-executioner in his jurisdiction, which usually covered tens of thousands of square miles.

The judicial apparatus was similarly plagued by a lack of professional competence. Judge Bean's whimsical rulings were Solomonic compared to what was happening in other courtrooms in the West. The local magistrates were responsible to the federal justices, but only on paper. The federal judges reserved for themselves the most serious cases (even if they did not fall directly under federal jurisdiction) as a means of depoliticizing the judicial process in the western territories.

Thus, Federal Judge Isaac C. Parker, appointed by President Grant to preside over the Western District of Arkansas, heard many cases involving charges of homicide. He ruled so severely that he became known as "the hanging judge." But a more careful look shows that Parker assumed control of cases when a federal marshal or deputy was killed—in the twenty-one years of his tenure, sixty-five such lawmen were killed in the line of duty. He also presided when the killing took place in federally controlled Indian Territory or when

*Stephen F. Austin,
the Father of Texas,
in a Norman Price
engraving after a
painting in the Texas
State Capitol, Austin.*

there was a real possibility that a local justice would be intimidated or corrupted. Of the 168 people Parker sentenced to death, only eighty-eight were actually hanged. The others were spared, in many instances because of the questions raised by just this issue of the federal court's jurisdiction in homicide cases. (Parker's reputation as a sadistic maniac was largely the work of a disgruntled defense lawyer, S.W. Harman, who had lost his share of cases tried before Judge Parker. Harman wrote a scathing book about the judge two years after Parker's death in 1896.)

What is clear from all this is that creating a system of law of any kind, however imperfect, in the Old West was as heroic an endeavor as finding a trail through the wilderness, fighting off the Indians, or any of the more physical acts we associate with heroism. For all the lawlessness attributed to the Old West (and there was a lot), the fact is that the story of the West is one of the triumph of these heroes of the law in establishing a peaceful environment in which the culture and the community could grow.

"Show me a hero," said F. Scott Fitzgerald, "and I'll write you a tragedy." Many of the stories that appear in this chapter do not end well. Often, the commitment to the law was only a temporary phase in people's otherwise violent and less-than-exemplary lives. And all too often, the energies of these heroes were spent on the frontier, and the pure pursuit of justice gave way to the political necessities of a growing economy. Gunfighters had a clear sense that their fate would be to die at the hand of the law; lawmen had a similar belief that their sacrifices would ultimately go unappreciated and unrewarded.

The heroes fall into two categories: the ones who opened the West, which included the fighters at the Alamo and the leaders of the wars for Texas independence, and the lawmen who made that West inhabitable. If there seems to be an emphasis on Texas in this chapter, it is because in Texas the conflicting forces of justice, independence, law, lawlessness, security, and unfettered individuality all came together into a maelstrom of activity after the Civil War—long after the rest of the West had been tamed by the forces of civilization. Many Texans will tell you (right to the present day) that they would not have it any other way.

STEPHEN AUSTIN

Stephen Fuller Austin is known as the Father of Texas, although he did not fare all that well when the time came for Texas to show its appreciation. He had continued the work of his father, Moses Austin, who began the political process of wresting Texas away from Spanish and Mexican authorities before Stephen entered the scene. But Stephen Austin was eclipsed by another hero, Sam Houston, who rose in the eyes of Texans as the leader of the forces in the battle that resulted in the independence of Texas. When Texas became an independent republic (albeit clearly anticipating entering the Union), Houston was elected president, and Austin accepted the position of secretary of state.

When Moses Austin died in 1821, he had already arranged a grant from the Spanish governor ceding 200,000 acres of Texas territory on which he could settle three hundred families. He had obtained a similar grant in 1798, and from that grant came a successful mining operation that enriched the coffers of the Spanish government, and, of course, the Austin family. The family fortunes were in a shambles, however, after the War of 1812, which prompted Moses Austin to appeal once again to the Spanish authorities. At the time, Stephen was a member of the legislature of Missouri territory. But when Moses died and Stephen took over the mantle of leadership of the project, he approached the matter with vigor (which turned out to be essential, since not every *t* had been crossed in the agreement with the Spanish government in San Antonio de Bexar).

Stephen Austin selected a site at the confluence of the Colorado and Brazos rivers, and the settlers began arriving by the end of 1821. When Mexico gained its independence from Spain (also in 1821), it did not enjoy a clean break from the mother country. As a result, although the new Mexican government was not happy about the American settlers on its land (having a clearer appreciation of America's long-range goals than, perhaps, the Spanish government had), the

The reading of the Texas Declaration of Independence in March 1836. Texas declared itself an independent republic even though Texans' goal from the very start was to become part of the United States. That goal was not realized until December 1845.

The multitalented Stephen Austin, who is still revered as one of Texas's greatest heroes.

among recent arrivals were settlers and who was simply there to conduct trade, something the Mexican government hoped to encourage. The new president of Mexico, Antonio Lopez de Santa Anna, was faced with a dilemma: the American colonists were developing the area and formed a diplomatic link to a possible ally, yet their precipitous growth made it clear that Americans were going to be a landed presence in Texas for many years to come. Austin could see only one solution to this situation: the creation of an American state within Mexico.

Austin was sent to Mexico City with a resolution for just this in 1835, and he presented it to the president; he was promptly arrested. After a year in prison assuring the authorities that his resolution was not meant as disloyalty (which required a fair bit of fancy arguing, for which his Yale education may have come in handy), Austin was released, and he returned to Texas. The news of his arrest had, in the meantime, inflamed Texas passions, and Austin had become a cause célèbre. Upon his return to Texas, he launched into a new role as the commander of American forces seeking independence from Mexico, the only course left open. In 1835 Austin successfully led his forces against the local Mexican garrison in San Antonio. Knowing that the Mexicans were going to retaliate, he went to Washington to seek the help of the American government. However, it was a bit early for the United States to get involved in the matter; the government's attention at the moment was focused on resolving the dispute it had with Mexico over the Florida peninsula.

Austin returned to Texas in June 1836, empty-handed, only to find that he had missed all the fireworks. In his absence, the battles of the Alamo and San Jacinto had taken place, and Texas had declared itself

need to shore up its borders against an expected attempt by Spain to recapture the country gave Austin an opening. In Mexico City, Austin was able to get favorable terms from the government that made him virtually the governor of the settled area.

By 1832 the original colony of three hundred families had grown to eight thousand, enough to start worrying the officials in Mexico City. The Mexican government had passed a law in 1830 limiting immigration from U.S. territory, but the isolation of the colony made it difficult to determine who

an independent republic. He ran for the presidency of the new country but was defeated by Sam Houston, the hero of the battles. Yet the Republic of Texas and the eventual settling of Texas and its admittance to statehood would not have come about had Stephen not assumed the burden of fulfilling his father's dream. Austin's biographers stress his diplomatic skills, but he was also a rugged frontiersman when the situation called for it. The colonies Austin created were usually situated in desolate areas with little in the way of farmland, mining resources, or, for that matter, any resources whatever. Austin died in December 1836 at the age of forty-three.

JUDGE ROY BEAN

Why is Roy Bean counted among the heroes of the American West? This question only improves with age, for as America becomes a society increasingly enmeshed in its own legal apparatus, the image of a vast frontier

in which the rule of law was determined by the often whimsical judgments of an illiterate saloon keeper tickles one's fancy. Bean was not by any means a champion of justice, and he was certainly not immune to being bribed or influenced or to making rulings that were beneficial to his own fortunes. But his homespun justice and the settling effect he had on western Texas make this man, who was called (mainly by himself) "the law west of the Pecos," an admirable figure. Many of the legends and stories told about Judge Roy Bean were originally told by Bean himself; he was his own best promoter.

Bean was born around 1825 in Kentucky. He left home in 1847 with his brother Sam and found himself in trouble in various

Lily Langtry, the object of Judge Roy Bean's obsession, never visited the town the judge named for her until after his death.

and cut Bean down. He was still alive, and the woman nursed him back to health. The rope left a permanent mark on Bean's neck, and he was never again able to turn his head. In all depictions of Bean, he is shown with a high collar that hides his neck. What the rope did to the blood-deprived cells in Bean's brain is anybody's guess.

During the Civil War, Bean operated a profitable blockade-running enterprise in New Mexico for the Confederacy, and after the war he continued to prosper in the San Antonio area. He was now married with a family. His wife, Virginia Chavez, was from the Canary Islands and was considered a highly cultured woman. When she left him in 1882, Bean sold everything, crossed the Pecos River, and set up a saloon in Vinegaroon, a tent city. He appointed himself justice of the peace and adjudicated disputes, often being accepted by the "litigants" only because of his good humor and the flowing whiskey. When Vinegaroon folded up, Bean moved to a desolate railroad station near the Rio Grande in west Texas. Because he had a lifelong admiration for the actress Lily Langtry, he named his saloon the Jersey Lilly (misspelled by the town sign painter) and he dubbed the town Langtry (although it's possible that the town was already called that before Bean's arrival). Having had a taste of the power involved in administering justice, he got himself elected justice of the peace and held court in the saloon, which he outfitted with a jury box and a witness stand. He often interrupted the proceedings to serve whiskey while he consulted his only law book: a tattered copy of the 1879 *Revised Statutes of Texas*.

The key to Bean's authority was the power of the Texas Rangers, the law enforcement group that dated back to Stephen Austin. Why they favored and supported his rulings is not clear; it may

places throughout the southwest. He killed a man in a duel over a woman in Chihuahua, Mexico, and escaped to San Diego and the protection of his brother Joshua. He spent some time in the San Diego jail (also for killing a man in a duel over a woman) and eventually wound up in San Gabriel, where Joshua had gone to set up a saloon. When Joshua was killed by the Spanish gunman Joaquin Murietta, Roy took over the saloon until he was arrested for (you guessed it) killing a man in a duel over a woman. Bean was taken by the dead man's friends, hanged, and left to die. After the lynching party left, the woman over whom the duel had been fought showed up

simply have been a matter of the alternative being anarchy. Bean had no grounding in law, to put it mildly (he once nearly had a lawyer hanged for using profanity in his courtroom when he uttered the phrase "habeas corpus"), and Stephen Austin would never have approved. Bean's courtroom was filled with homespun wisdom (or what passed for wisdom) mixed with the violent, unbridled temperament of the new state of Texas. Bean frequently used the power of the court to excuse terrible crimes by Texans against Mexicans and Chinese railroad workers. He once claimed that his law book indeed had laws against homicide, but said nothing about killing Chinese. On one occasion, he found a Texan innocent of killing a Mexican, claiming it was the Mexican who should be tried for stepping in front of where a Texan was shooting. Another time, Bean found forty dollars and a gun in the pocket of a dead man and promptly confiscated the money by fining the dead man forty dollars for carrying a concealed weapon. The courtroom of Judge Roy Bean became an attraction for railroad passengers passing through Texas.

Bean was finally kicked out of office in 1892 when the number of votes cast for him in an election was greater than the total number of citizens eligible to vote. Bean had, in fact, offended both law and reason many times before, so it's reasonable to assume that he was deposed when the Texas Rangers believed he no longer served a purpose. In 1896 Bean sponsored a championship boxing match between Bob Fitzsimmons and Peter Maher. Boxing was illegal in Texas at the time, so Bean staged the fight on a barge in the middle of the Rio Grande, with spectators packing both banks of the river. The event was not only profitable, but also enhanced Bean's reputation for outlandish entertainment.

Bean's infatuation with Lily Langtry took the form of years of fan letters, photos of the actress around the courtroom (including a tattered photograph that Bean kept in his pocket and would take out and smile at when the testimony got slow), and annual Christmas cards. It was his lifelong dream to meet Langtry, and he came close in 1888, when he saw her perform in a San Antonio playhouse. For reasons still unclear, he never met her, and he returned to Langtry, where he died on March 16, 1903. Lily Langtry passed through Langtry, Texas, a year later and was presented with a gun said to have belonged to the judge.

The classic biography of Bean is C.L. Sonnischen's *Roy Bean: Law West of the Pecos*, published in 1943. Bean has appeared in several movies as a minor character (whenever a boozing, stereotypical judge was called for), but received two elaborate portrayals in film that have added much to his legendary status in American culture. The first was the William Wyler film *The Westerner*, in which a cowhand, played by Gary Cooper, is falsely accused of stealing a horse and is brought before Judge Roy Bean, played by Walter Brennan. The cowboy is aware of the judge's infatuation with

The shoot-out scene from The Life and Times of Judge Roy Bean, *a film that was only loosely based on the life of Judge Bean and that featured Paul Newman in the title role.*

Lily Langtry, and saves himself from the hangman's noose by implying that he knows Langtry and may be able to obtain a lock of the famous actress's hair for the judge. The cowboy escapes, and Judge Bean finally gets to meet Langtry in a theater in which she is performing and in which Bean is the only audience member because he has bought out the entire theater. Brennan received an Oscar for his portrayal. Even though Cooper plays the hero who returns to topple the judge (the shoot-out takes place in the empty theater in which Bean has been sitting watching Langtry), the picture is really about a mean-spirited dispenser of unreasoned judgments who still managed to keep the Old West from becoming a jungle.

Bean was a perfect character for the humorous western films of the 1970s. He was portrayed by Paul Newman in the 1972 film *The Life and Times of Judge Roy Bean*, directed by John Huston and written by John Milius. Newman's portrayal is compelling but much too sanitized to bear any real resemblance to the historical figure. (Ava Gardner's portrayal of Lily Langtry turned out to be the most praised performance in the film.) It has been suggested that the true story of Judge Roy Bean and his rule of law west of the Pecos has yet to be told.

BUFFALO BILL CODY

Most of what the world once knew about the Old West was due in large part to the career of one man: William Frederick Cody, known to all as Buffalo Bill. Cody was a genuine part of the Old West (or "Wild West," as he called it). After a remarkable career as a scout, soldier, and frontiersman, Cody spent a great deal of time conveying a flavor of the Old West to audiences on both sides of the Atlantic. To regard Buffalo Bill Cody as a mere showman would be to miss the importance of his influence on historical developments. It would also be a failure to realize that before Cody there was no well-established image of the West. Cody didn't have an enlightened attitude toward the Indians—certainly not by today's standards. But he did show respect to Sitting Bull, and he used Indians in his Wild West show in a dignified way. (He also made a point of treating the Indians he employed well, at least while they were in his employ.)

William Cody was born in Iowa in 1846, the fourth of eight children. In 1850 the family moved to Kansas, where Isaac Cody, William's father, set up a sawmill. In 1854 Isaac was stabbed while speaking in favor of making Kansas a free state (barring slavery), and though he did not die right then, the family blamed his death in 1857 on the wounds sustained in the stabbing. Young William took a job as a messenger for the Russell, Majors, and Waddell freight-carry-

Buffalo Bill Cody posed with Chief Sitting Bull in Montreal in 1880. His "Congress of Rough Riders" brought a sense of the West, albeit skewed and romanticized, to many easterners and Canadians—and even to Europeans abroad.

Around the world, posters like this one would announce the coming of Buffalo Bill Cody's Wild West show before it arrived in a town or city.

ing company. When the company established the Pony Express, he became one of the more celebrated riders of the difficult Julesburg run. It was during this period that Cody met Wild Bill Hickok, and the two became lifelong friends.

In 1861 he returned home, where he became part of the jayhawker bands who terrorized pro-Confederate communities while stealing horses throughout Kansas. He eventually joined the Seventh Kansas Volunteer Cavalry and served in the Civil War. After the war, Cody, now married (to Louisa "Lulu" Frederici, whom he had met during the war), tried his hand at hotel-keeping, but soon realized he was meant for the open spaces of the West. In 1867 he landed a contract to provide buffalo meat for the workers of the Union Pacific Railroad, which resulted in his being given the name Buffalo Bill. This moniker had already been given to a man named Comstock but was transferred to Cody when he bettered Comstock's single-day record for buffalo kills: sixty-nine vs. forty-six.

Buffalo Bill's knowledge of buffalo country gave him the perfect background to serve as Philip Sheridan's scout, and he served in that capacity for four years, longer than any other scout. He was part of General Eugene Carr's military campaign of 1869 against the Cheyenne. Carr made a special request of the War Department that Cody be paid more for his services during the campaign. Cody also acted as a guide for a number of celebrated hunting parties, such as the one conducted by the Russian Grand Duke Alexis in 1872. It was during that year that Cody met Edward Judson, who wrote dime novels under the pen name Ned Buntline. The successful author soon convinced Cody to stage a melodrama about the West on the Chicago stage. Cody stayed on the stage for eleven seasons, spending the off-season hunting and fighting in Indian country. Legend had him as the man who killed Yellow Hand, known as the "first scalp [in revenge] for Custer," in a much publicized duel that never actually took place.

Cody organized his Wild West show in 1883, running it successfully for four years before taking it to London in 1887 for Queen Victoria's Jubilee, where it created a sensation. The show toured Europe, drawing wildly enthusiastic crowds, and then scored its greatest success as part of the Chicago World's Columbian Exposition in 1893. At different times, the show featured Sitting Bull; the sharp-shooting, trick-riding Annie Oakley; and Buck Taylor, "King of the Cowboys." It also included live buffalo, which turned out to be fortunate because all the modern herds that have survived are from the stock used in Cody's shows. (Although Cody was a buffalo hunter, he hunted buffalo only for meat. The thinning out and eventual destruction of the buffalo on the plains was the work of pelt hunters, who were allowed to hunt without restriction as part of the government's anti-Indian policy.) The two highlights of the show—Custer's Last Stand and the Robbery of the Deadwood Stagecoach—became staples of all Wild West shows, probably to the present day. The show continued for thirty years, often under the direction of Cody's partner, Nate Salsbury, and, after Nate's death in 1902, under Gordon Lillie, who was known as "Pawnee Bill."

Cody offered and paid for the services of some of his Indian performers to General Nelson Miles when he was hunting Geronimo. Cody's men not only spoke English, but also understood the ways of whites at least as well, if not better, than Miles understood Indians. Cody was awarded the Congressional Medal of Honor in 1872, but then, strangely enough, he was asked to return it when Congress ruled that it could be given only to members of the U.S. Army.

While Cody was touring in England, he met and fell in love with an English actress named Katherine Clemmons and planned to marry her just as soon as he could divorce Lulu. Back home Mrs. Cody proved a formidable foe in court, however, and she held up the proceedings until Clemmons gave up and married someone else. Although Cody made a large fortune performing, he was also a very big spender: he invested eighty thousand dollars in Katherine Clemmons's career as a gift. As a result, Cody died poor. He spent the last months of his life in a virtual stupor at his sister's home in Virginia. He died on January 10, 1917—the story was front-page news worldwide.

Buffalo Bill was made into a larger-than-life figure largely through the efforts of Ned Buntline, who became interested in Cody when he was turned down by Frank North, another famous frontiersman. Buntline wrote about Cody for years even after they fell out (which irritated Cody, though there was nothing he could do about it). The character of Buffalo Bill appeared in many serials in newspapers and in scores of dime novels. After some fifty years of publications about Cody, much of it directed by him or derived from publicity connected to his show business enterprises, a genuinely researched biog-

Whatever one may think of Cody's exploitation of the Indians in his show, he took pains to use and preserve genuine Indian artifacts and garb. In this picture, the two Native Americans on the right are joined by a white woman dressed as an Indian on the left.

when it was adapted for film, as *Buffalo Bill and the Indians; Or, Sitting Bull's History Lesson*, directed by Robert Altman, it took on a bizarre, black-comic quality with Paul Newman as a manic Buffalo Bill.

There has never been a serious attempt to look at Cody as anything but a social stereotype. This is all the more remarkable because the western as a genre has been written off as dead and buried a number of times over the past thirty years, only to be revived and renewed with greater (or lesser) insight.

DAVY CROCKETT

There could hardly be a hero of the American West better known or more admired than David "Davy" Crockett. The main reasons surely must be his exploits as a wilderness tracker and his legendary courage at the Battle of the Alamo. Walt Disney's Sunday night programs in the 1950s certainly went a long way in bringing the historical Crockett to the attention of American television viewers. Although Disney took generous license with some of the details, combining all the legends and tall tales with the historical record in an entertaining amalgam, at least everything had some connection to Davy Crockett, real or legendary.

Much of Davy's image is the product of tall tales he himself told, openly admitting he was exaggerating to amuse his colleagues in Congress or the Tennessee legislature. An accomplished yarn spinner who was possessed of a particularly warm personality, Davy was beloved, admired, respected, and sought after wherever he went. This, of course, also made him a

Davy Crockett in a portrait by J.G. Chapman, as he is usually remembered: a frontiersman with a broad smile and a grand gesture.

raphy was written by Don Russell and published as *The Lives and Legends of Buffalo Bill* in 1960.

Buffalo Bill made unimportant and largely unhistorical appearances in several pre–World War II films, such as De Mille's *The Plainsman*, and in several films that focused on Annie Oakley (most notably in the 1935 George Stevens film, *Annie Oakley*, in which Moroni Olsen plays an interesting Buffalo Bill to Barbara Stanwyck's somewhat cardboard Annie). In 1969, a Broadway play by Arthur Kopit appeared with the title *Indians*; it portrayed Sitting Bull as tortured and exploited in Cody's Wild West show. The play was in keeping with the social consciousness of the period, but

formidable opponent, and had he been just a bit more thick-skinned, he would have been able to play the political games that were the daily fare in Washington (no less a century ago than today).

Crockett was born on August 17, 1786, in eastern Tennessee, to John and Rebecca Crockett, who had come from Virginia a few years earlier. As a youngster, Davy showed little interest in school, choosing instead to work as a cattle driver and farm laborer. On October 24, 1805, he thought he was going to be marrying his childhood sweetheart, Margaret Elder, and he even paid for a marriage license in the morning. But later that day Elder wound up marrying someone else. The following August Davy married Polly Finley in a rousing frontier wedding.

The Crocketts moved to Tennessee and settled near Franklin in 1811. Davy joined Andrew Jackson's militia in the campaign against the Creek Indians in Alabama, but was not involved in the famous battle at Horseshoe Bend. He also served in the Tennessee Mounted Gunmen under Major Russell, fighting in Florida but not in the Battle of Fort Barancas, and with Andrew Jackson in Alabama, but not at the Battle of New Orleans. He returned home stricken with malaria contracted in Florida—he was to suffer bouts of the disease throughout his life—and moved his family to the western part of the state.

After Polly died in 1816, Crockett married the widow Elizabeth Patton and moved deeper into the Tennessee wilderness. He was elected to the Tennessee legislature in 1820 (as a result of a prank played on him by some friends) and again in 1823. In 1825 he ran for Congress and was defeated, but he was elected in 1827, reelected in 1829, defeated in 1831, and then reelected in 1833. Crockett was a controversial member of Congress because he supported the liberal fiscal policies of the Bank of the United States, opposed by Jackson, that would permit settlers to borrow federal money for developing the frontier. He also opposed the Jacksonian candidate for the senate, which did not endear him to the Jackson administration.

Celebrated in Washington society as the "Coonskin Congressman," and entertaining easterners with his humorous tall tales, Crockett was a formidable challenge to Jackson and was even being considered as a possible presidential candidate of the Whig party. The Democrats targeted Crockett in the election of 1835. The previous year, Crockett had been invited to tour eastern industrial areas looking for possible developers of western lands, including Tennessee. The tour turned out to be a ruse to get him out of the capital and to allow his opponents to charge him with neglecting his duties in Washington. In a campaign that drew national attention, Crockett lost his seat. "You can all go to hell," he was quoted as saying, "I'm going to Texas."

On November 1, 1835, Crockett and five companions set out to explore Texas. The group arrived in San Antonio in February 1836, and Crockett, along with a dozen

The Battle of the Alamo was a heroic defeat and strategically unimportant, but it provided the psychological impetus for the Texas War for Independence.

Celebrated in Washington as a raconteur without equal, Crockett was a favorite at the table of Andrew Jackson.

Tennesseean volunteers, joined the forces at the Alamo, the mission named after the cottonwood trees that grew in the grove outside the mission walls. The fort was then in the thick of preparing for a spring encounter with the Mexican army. The Texans, Davy discovered, were not all of one mind at the time. Sam Houston, who was in charge of the Texas regular army, wanted to stage a guerrilla war against the Mexicans, figuring that was the only chance they had against the much larger Mexican army. James Fannin, who was commanding a small contingent at Goliad, ninety-five miles south of the Alamo, wanted to launch an attack on the Mexican garrison at Matamoros, believing they would catch the Mexicans off guard. In command at the Alamo was Colonel William B. Travis, a lawyer who had been involved in the Texas independence movement since its beginning. He had arrived a month earlier with thirty regulars to join the 120 men already at the Alamo.

Houston sent word with the famed frontiersman Jim Bowie that Travis should abandon the mission, but Bowie found the Alamo battle-ready, so he decided to stay there and join the fight. Bowie was in the final stages of a long bout with tuberculosis, and he knew that he did not have long to live. The men voted Bowie in command, even though he was a volunteer. (Apparently, Travis impressed the men as a bit too bookish, and was not the fighter Jim Bowie was.) Later, with Bowie bedridden by his illness, the two men agreed to share command.

On February 1, General Santa Anna mobilized his army and set out for Texas; on the 16th he crossed the Rio Grande. The Mexican army that attacked the Alamo consisted of fifty-four hundred men and twenty-one cannon. Travis believed the wet plains would slow Santa Anna down and that an attack would not come until spring, but by February 20 the Mexicans were within fifty miles of San Antonio. Travis sent out a messenger to Goliad asking Fannin to send reinforcements, but the group at Goliad had dug in and were waiting for an attack.

The preparations for the attack were intense, and every hand prepared gunpowder and cannon ammunition out of horseshoes and any other metal that could be found. Eighteen cannon emplacements were set up around the perimeter by Green Jameson. Santa Anna was going to attack on February 21, but a rainstorm the night before delayed the attack. The Texans locked themselves inside the Alamo compound while the other people of San Antonio fled the town. The 150 men and 25 women and an unknown (but small) number of children looked out at the great Mexican army and saw, hanging from the San Antonio church, a red flag hoisted by Santa Anna, which meant that no prisoners would be taken. Travis sent another messenger out for help, and shot off a cannon blast at the red flag in reply—it would indeed be a battle to the death.

On the morning of February 24, the Mexican army dug in about four hundred yards (365.8m) from the Alamo and began shelling the fort with cannon fire. Again Travis sent a messenger for help (this time the messenger just barely snuck through the Mexican lines). Fannin was inclined to send help this time, but disorganization in his camp delayed the reinforcements' departure until they figured it was already too late. Meanwhile, the commander at Gonzales, George Kimball, had received one of Travis's appeals and arrived at the Alamo with another twenty-five men on March 1. Inside the Alamo, between engagements, Davy Crockett was said to have played a fiddle while John McGregor, a Scot, played bagpipes. By March 5, the Mexican army had advanced to new trenches only two hundred yards (182.9m) away, and the Texans inside the Alamo sensed that their time was up.

In a scene that has become an indelible part of American lore (even though it did not appear in print until fifty years after the battle), Colonel Travis gathered everyone in the courtyard during a lull in the fighting and drew a line in the sand. He asked everyone who wished to stay and fight to cross the line. Anyone else was free to attempt an escape. Everyone except a Frenchman named Louis Rose crossed the line; Jim Bowie asked that his cot be carried across because he was too sick to make it on his own.

The final attack came in the early morning hours of March 6. It began at about five o'clock and lasted ninety minutes. In the end, it was said that Crockett, having run out of ammunition, swung his rifle, "Old Betsy," like a club until he was cut down by

For some, the greatest hero of the Alamo was Jim Bowie, who fought the Mexicans while near delirium on his deathbed. This engraving, called The Death of Jim Bowie, *was reproduced often in the many tellings of the Battle of the Alamo.*

a bayonet. (Another version had it that he was captured alive by Santa Anna and tortured to death.) The Mexicans went through the Alamo killing everyone except Susannah Dickerson, whose friend had pleaded with Santa Anna the night before to let her live. The soldiers found Dickerson clutching her young daughter, Angelina, and brought them to Santa Anna. Santa Anna told Dickerson she could leave, so that she could tell the story to other Texans as a warning of what armed resistance would bring.

Dickerson and her daughter went to Gonzales and told the Texans there the story of the Alamo. The Mexicans had lost fifteen hundred men in the battle; the Texans had lost only 180. The tale had the opposite effect of what Santa Anna had hoped for. "Remember the Alamo" became a battle cry for Texas independence and was directly responsible for the victory of Sam Houston at the Battle of San Jacinto, one of the most lopsided victories in all military history.

Many legends about Davy and his trusty rifle, "Old Betsy," entered the American folk tradition and were included in a publication known as *Davy Crockett's Almanack*, a periodical that was the forerunner of the twentieth-century comic book. The first edition appeared in 1836, and the *Almanack* was published for more than forty years, becoming one of the most successful American publishing ventures of the nineteenth century.

Davy Crockett has been portrayed several times in movies, mostly in films about the Battle of the Alamo. But the Disney television series *Davy Crockett: King of the Wild Frontier*, which was released as a feature film in 1956, devoted one third of its length to his career in Congress, one third to his wilderness days, and one third to the Alamo. Fess Parker's portrayal became the

Sam Houston, the hero of the Battle of San Jacinto.

standard by which any other portrayal of a wilderness frontiersman is measured. The larger-than-life renderings given by John Wayne in the 1960 epic *The Alamo* (which Wayne produced, financed, and directed, and which drove him to bankruptcy and forced him out of retirement) and by Brian Keith in the 1987 made-for-cable-television *The Alamo: 13 Days of Glory* were far from historical. And Arthur Hunnicut's folksy, innocent interpretation in the 1955 film *The Last Command* was also far from historical.

SAM HOUSTON

With all the larger-than-life characters running around Texas before the Civil War, it is hard to imagine that one person could come along and dwarf the rest, yet that is exactly what happened with the greatest Texan of them all, Sam Houston. Before Houston became the greatest Texan, he was already a great Tennesseean. Born in Virginia on March 2, 1793, he was raised in Tennessee, where he became very familiar with the Cherokee Indians and even lived with them for a while (he was given the name "the Raven" by the tribe). He fought with Andrew Jackson in 1813, and the two men became lifelong friends. After completing a law course, he became the district attorney of Nashville and was twice elected to Congress, in 1823 and 1825. Houston was then twice elected governor of Tennessee, but in 1829 his wife left him, and he resigned from office in the middle of his second term.

Houston went to live with the Cherokees in Arkansas and took a Cherokee woman as his wife. He became a spokesman for the

Sam Houston (on the right), dicussing military tactics with a lieutenant. Houston was a large man with large appetites.

were killed; another 730 were wounded or captured. Two Texan soldiers were killed during the battle, and thirty died over the next few days from wounds suffered during the battle—in all, thirty-two Texans died. Santa Anna himself was caught trying to escape disguised as a beggar. He was brought to Sam Houston, who had been shot in the ankle during the fray. "Remember the Alamo" had been the rallying cry of the Texans since Santa Anna's army had massacred the Texans who defended the San Antonio mission fort. This would have been the perfect time to seek revenge for the Alamo, but Houston decided to show mercy. He shipped Santa Anna to Washington in hopes of gaining for Texas the real prize he was seeking: not independence, but American statehood.

Houston, now a hero, was elected first president of the Lone Star Republic, and then was the first senator to represent Texas in Congress. In 1861 Houston, a Unionist, refused to go along with the state's allegiance to the Confederacy, so he retired from public life to his farm near Huntsville. He died there on July 26, 1863.

Houston was a robust man who stood over six feet tall and had large appetites. He was a boisterous man who was accepted and admired in the halls of Congress, in the teepees of the Cherokee, and as commander in chief of the Texas army. He married for a third time in 1840, and he was happy in this marriage until his death. It is a testament to the reverence in which he was held by his fellow Texans that he was reelected governor in 1859, even though he opposed the nearly universally held desire among Texans for secession.

Coming out of the Battle of San Jacinto, in addition to Texas independence, is the story behind the song "The Yellow Rose of Texas," one of the most popular American folk songs. The story concerns a mulatto

Cherokees in Washington and was sent to Texas by Jackson to observe and report on Indian matters. He quickly became involved in the movement for Texas independence. When the split with Mexico came in March 1836, he was one of the signers of the Texas Declaration of Independence and was made commander in chief of the Texas army. Although he raised a force of eight hundred men, many people were skeptical of Houston's leadership.

A month and a half after the Battle of the Alamo, on April 21, 1836, Houston staged a bold mid-siesta surprise attack on the army of Santa Anna camped at San Jacinto. About half of the Mexican force—630 soldiers—

slave girl named Emily Morgan who was taken by Santa Anna when he overran the Morgan ranch. Legend has it that Sam Houston's forces were able to achieve such a lopsided victory because Santa Anna was busy romancing Emily in his tent at the time of the attack.

WILD BILL HICKOK

The lawmen who were heroes of the West did not always have choirboy backgrounds. For every outlaw who was reputed to come from a churchgoing, God-fearing family of ministers and Sunday-school teachers, there was a lawman who had a shady past on the wrong side of the law—and sometimes even on the wrong side of the hangman's noose. The best of these lawmen had hot tempers and itchy trigger fingers; they were not above settling an argument quickly with a well-placed bullet to the head. The image that is often portrayed of the local sheriff or the marshal being a calm rock of cool reason (an image that James Arness took to an almost sleep-inducing degree in his portrayal of the unflappable Marshal Matt Dillon in the long-running television series *Gunsmoke*) is, sad to say, a twentieth-century invention. The career of James Butler Hickok, better known throughout the West and in legend as "Wild Bill Hickok," is a perfect example.

James Butler Hickok was born in Illinois in 1837, the son of an ardent believer in the abolitionist cause who actively ran an underground railroad, helping runaway slaves escape bounty hunters. There are several fanciful stories about how he received the nickname "Wild Bill." In all

likelihood, it derived either from early attempts to differentiate him from his brother, Lorenzo, who was known since his youth as "Tame Bill," or it was the name an unknowing bystander yelled out when Hickok single-handedly prevented a lynching party from killing a man he believed innocent, one of the early legendary exploits for which Hickok gained fame.

He served on the Union side during the Civil War, sometimes as a scout and other times as a spy. He was briefly a scout for Custer's Seventh Cavalry, and eventually became a deputy marshal. Hickok's legend began (as many legends do) with his just barely escaping a life-and-death struggle

An unusual photo of Wild Bill Hickok wearing a fur hat.

A rare photo of several western heroes assembled together. From left: Charley Utter, Wild Bill Hickok, Buffalo Bill Cody, Texas Jack Omohundro, and an unidentified cowboy.

with a bear. He killed the bear with a Bowie knife, and he was nursed back from the brink of death. He was in his twenties, and he recovered while working as a stablehand in a Nebraska stagecoach station. In July 1861 Dave McCanles (a married man who was seeing Hickok's girlfriend, Sara Shill, on the side) came to the stagecoach station and challenged Hickok to fight him—for some reason, everyone regarded McCanles as the injured party in this affair. Hickok refused, and when McCanles and some of his buddies stormed the house, Hickok shot them, while the station owner and Hickok's boss, Horace Wellman, took care of McCanles's cohorts outside, somehow killing them with a hoe.

Throughout Hickok's adult life, he found himself in similar circumstances again and again—fighting over a woman or settling an argument with a gun—with the result that, proficient a gunfighter as he was, he

did not live to see his fortieth birthday. In Springfield, Missouri, Hickok fought a duel with Dave Tutt in the summer of 1865 over the affections of Susanna Moore; he was tried after killing Tutt and was acquitted. In 1869 Hickok was already serving as a law-man in Hays City, Kansas, and showed him-self to be anything but timid about using a gun to end a drunken brawl or deal with anyone resisting arrest. He used these quick-gun tactics in July 1870 to break up a brawl involving soldiers from the Seventh Cavalry; one of these men was Tom Custer, the general's brother. Custer brought a group of soldiers to town the next day with the intention of tearing Hickok limb from limb, but the lawman had the sense to make himself scarce.

Wild Bill Hickok's most famous gunfight took place in October 1871, when he was marshal of Abilene, Kansas. After quelling a group of rowdies led by the coarse Phil

Coe in the local saloon, Hickok heard a shot, and when he went to investigate he found Coe standing with a gun in his hand. Thinking Coe had shot his deputy, Mike Williams, Hickok drew his guns and shot Coe in the stomach, sustaining a bullet in the leg from Coe's gun. Just then, a man who had been waiting at the Abilene train station and who had heard the shooting burst into the saloon, thinking the sheriff might need his help. The wounded Hickok whirled and shot the man twice in the head before realizing it was his friend and deputy, Williams. Hickok was devastated by the error and closed down the town for a lavish funeral for Williams.

Both Hickok's eyesight and his fortunes began to fail after the death of Williams. He wandered through the West, sometimes suffering the indignity of having to back down from a challenge by a younger, faster gunfighter looking to make a quick reputation. And just as often he spent the night sleeping off a drunk in the local jail. In 1876, after many years of womanizing across the West, he married Agnes Lake, owner of a Wild West circus, and settled in the town of Deadwood, a mining community in Dakota Territory, hoping to make a fortune as a gambler.

Hickok was not much of a gambler, however, and he was almost always deep in debt. On August 2, 1876, Hickok was in a card game with three other gamblers, and was sitting with his back to the door, Several times he had tried to convince the player with his back to the wall, Frank Massie, to change places with him, but Massie just laughed him off. During the game, Jack McCall, a card player who had lost $110 to Hickok the day before, came into the saloon, walked up to the bar and had a whiskey, and then calmly stationed himself behind Hickok, presumably to watch the game. But McCall drew his .45

and shot Hickok in the back of the head. There was evidence that McCall had been paid $200 by Hickok's enemies to kill him. McCall was tried and hanged for the murder, and the hand Hickok was holding when he was shot—a pair of aces, a pair of eights, and a queen—became known as "dead man's hand."

In his travels, Hickok made the acquaintance of a remarkable number of legendary figures in the history and lore of the West. He was a friend of Buffalo Bill Cody and he accompanied Cody on his royal Russian buffalo hunt in 1872 and appeared with him onstage back east in a Ned Buntline play, *Scouts of the Plains*. In 1867 he met the journalist Henry Morton Stanley (who became world-famous for finding Livingstone in Africa). The articles Stanley wrote about Hickok, mixing fact and fiction, both generously supplied by Hickok, appeared in the *New York Tribune*. It was because of these articles, as well as an article by Colonel George Ward Nichols for *Harper's New Monthly Magazine*, that Hickok became known as the "Prince of Pistoleers," making Hickok a legend of the West for years to come. Hickok also met, and perhaps even married, "Calamity Jane" (Martha Jane Canary); he almost certainly had a daughter by her.

During some parts of his life, he was a lawman; during other times he was an outlaw—either way, Wild Bill Hickok was quick with a gun and used it to get whatever he wanted.

This 1867 engraving depicts an episode that was repeated many times in Wild Bill Hickok's life. With only Wild Bill standing between order and chaos, many bandits made a concerted effort to kill him before embarking on their crime sprees. No wonder he was so wild.

Wild Bill Hickok was six feet tall and had shoulder-length hair. He was fastidious about his clothes and appearance: he wore fashionable city clothes or dashing buckskins and made a point of bathing every day (an unusual practice on the frontier). He was quiet and courteous, and did not change his demeanor even in the midst of a gunfight. His cool manner while engaged in the bloody business of killing people has led some observers to question his mental stability, but these views often ignore the context of the times and the violent environment in which Hickok lived. Hickok was famous for carrying two pearl-handled Colt .45 pistols in his belt (not, as usually depicted, in holsters, which were uncommon outside of Texas), with the handles facing forward.

Wild Bill Hickok appeared in many dime novels, filling the role of the fast-shooting lawman whenever called for. His connection with many famous people of the West—Custer, Buffalo Bill, Calamity Jane—made him a character in any story involving them. Books about the life and times of Wild Bill Hickok have been among the best and

most authentic of the period (virtually every western character provided the basis for lurid and sensationalistic literature about the West). Joseph G. Rosa's *They Called Him Wild Bill: The Life and Adventures of James Butler Hickok* is that rare gem: an exciting read that is meticulously detailed and researched. Recent studies of the lawmen of the West indicate that they may have been no more balanced (or less psychotic) than the gunslinging outlaws that became hunted villains. Whether or not this new version will hold up, only time will tell, but the steadying effect the lawmen had on the social environment is not disputed. That the ordinary citizen had only the law enforcer to turn to when victimized by violent bandits or rustlers meant that the civilizing forces at play in the West had a chance to take hold.

The film portrayals of Wild Bill Hickok came early, with his name (if not his character) appearing in many early "oater" one- and two-reel silent westerns. A character of such renown was not likely to escape the attention of actor-filmmaker William S. Hart, and his portrayal in the lead role of the 1923 film *Wild Bill Hickok* was, like many of Hart's efforts, a well-intentioned, careful, if somewhat romanticized presentation of the facts. Hart changed some of the details of the story line in deference to living relatives of characters in the film, but for the period, the film was remarkably ahead of its time.

Because of his wide range of activities, portrayals of Wild Bill Hickok were influenced by the dramatic requirements of specific story lines instead of the historical realities. In De Mille's *The Plainsman*, a 1936 epic about Custer, Hickok is portrayed by Gary Cooper as a dapper scout helping Custer stop gunrunners from arming the Indians. Hickok was portrayed by such actors as Richard Dix in the 1941 film *Badlands of Dakota* and a dashing Howard

Keel in the 1953 biopic *Calamity Jane*. An interesting and somewhat odd rendering was given by Charles Bronson in the 1977 film *The White Buffalo*, in which Hickok is portrayed as haunted by fears of death, symbolized by a white buffalo that runs through his dreams. Jeff Corey's brief portrayal of Hickok in Arthur Penn's 1970 classic *Little Big Man* was probably the most authentic.

The most widely known portrayal of Hickok, however, was Guy Madison's in the popular television program *The Adventures of Wild Bill Hickok*. This show, which aired from 1951 to 1958, was sometimes a full hour in length and was among the first to be regularly broadcast in color. Madison was groomed better than probably any man who ever lived in the Old West, which served as a contrast to his disheveled sidekick, the purely fictional Jingles, played by Andy ("Hey, Wild Bill, wait for me!") Devine. Madison's Hickok, with his guns backward (but in holsters), became the model for lawmen and heroes for practically all subsequent television westerns.

WYATT EARP

THE EARP BROTHERS, AND DOC HOLLIDAY

There is arguably no other figure of the Old West who has endured in the popular mind as a wearer of the hero's white hat like Wyatt Earp. The incident in which Wyatt, his brothers Morgan and Virgil, and Doc Holliday found a lasting place in American folklore—the gunfight at the O.K. Corral—lasted less than a minute

and was, on the face of it, an ordinary occurrence in the life of the American West. Yet it catapulted the names of both the victors—the Earps and Doc Holliday—and the vanquished—the McLaury brothers, the Clantons, and Billy Claiborne—into the collective American memory to a level far beyond their actual importance in history. The Earps, in fact, were not particularly lionized in their own day (in the way Wild Bill Hickok, for example, was) and did not achieve fame until the 1920s with the publication of books by Walter Noble Burns and Stuart N. Lake.

Burns and Lake did not have the last word, however, and to the present day, different views have been advanced about the

An 1882 photo of Wyatt Earp as marshal of Dodge City.

Earp brothers, some regarding them as heroes, others as violent frauds. Even a cursory look at the basic facts reveals the kind of ambiguities that could (and did) spawn a cottage industry. The clean-cut image of the dedicated lawman with blazing speed on the draw, which was how Hugh O'Brien portrayed Wyatt Earp on television, has become a cliché in American culture. The show may have been one of the most successful television westerns ever aired, but it certainly wasn't an accurate portrayal of Wyatt Earp.

The Earps were a close-knit Illinois family with seven children, all born between 1837 and 1857. They were all boys except the youngest, Adelia. The father, Nicholas Earp, moved across the face of the continent quite a bit during his life. The Earps can be included in the great mass of people who were motivated to move westward as much by a simple restlessness as by the hopes of economic betterment. In 1864 the family set out for California and settled in San Bernardino, with Virgil following later and joining them after a sojourn in Prescott, Arizona. For reasons that are still unclear, Nicholas moved the family again, this time back east, first to Monmouth, Illinois, their old stomping grounds, and then to Lamar, Missouri. Virgil and Wyatt straggled behind, working on the Union Pacific Railroad in Wyoming and then catching up to the family in Lamar.

In 1870 Wyatt married and ran for constable of Lamar, just beating his half-brother Newton. He apparently did a good job and would have remained there (in spite of problems he had with his in-laws), but in 1871 his wife died of typhoid. Wyatt was shattered by the loss and wandered through Indian Territory for months at a time, getting into one sort of trouble or another. In 1872 he was arrested for horse stealing, but he escaped to Kansas before

being tried. Two years later, he settled in Wichita, Kansas, where his brother James owned a saloon and a brothel. He was hired as a deputy there and seemed to be successful. But in 1875, when he got into a fist-fight with someone running against his boss, the marshal, the townspeople demanded that he be dismissed.

Wyatt had developed some skill as a gambler and occasionally supported himself with his winnings, but clearly the profession he took to most avidly was law enforcement. When he settled in Dodge City, Kansas, he spent some of the time gambling and some policing, with short spurts of prospecting in the Black Hills after gold had been found there. He served as the assistant marshal of Dodge City (a higher and more official designation than deputy) until 1879, forging friendships with many townspeople, including John Henry "Doc" Holliday, a gun-toting dentist; Luke Short, a saloon-keeping card-shark; and William Bartholomew "Bat" Masterson, a card-playing dandy with an adventurous spirit and a quick draw.

Wyatt had also remarried by 1879, and the following year he convinced his brothers, who were every bit as possessed as he with the Earp wanderlust, to settle in the boomtown of Tombstone, Arizona. In a short time, five Earp brothers had established themselves in Tombstone, many with jobs in law enforcement or as guards for Wells Fargo shipments. When the local marshal died in 1880, Virgil replaced him until a new marshal could be appointed. Meanwhile, Wyatt became a partner in the town's major entertainment establishment, the Oriental Saloon, and he brought Bat Masterson and Luke Short to town to work for him. The new marshal disappeared mysteriously one night in late 1880, and Virgil was appointed interim marshal once again. With various business and political ven-

The Dodge City Peace Commission that tamed and brought order to the Wild West town. From left: C. Bassett, W.W. Harris, Wyatt Earp, Luke Short, McNeal, Bat Masterson, and Neal Brown.

James D. "Doc" Holliday in the 1880s.

Virgil Earp in 1887.

1872, which made him a valuable professional wherever he went on the frontier. How he came to be on the frontier is unclear: it may have been because he had fired shots above the heads of a black family swimming on family property, or because he killed one of them, or because he was told that he had pulmonary tuberculosis and needed to live in a hotter, drier climate.

By 1872 Holliday had settled in Dallas, Texas, and had established a successful dental practice. He had, as was the case with many aristocratic southern gentlemen, a talent and flair for card playing. Although he was a successful gambler at the poker table in the Dallas saloons, it was only a matter of time before he found himself involved in one of the gunfights that were a gambler's occupational hazard. In 1875 he killed a man in a gambling dispute, and although he was not prosecuted, he left Dallas and began wandering through the Southwest, supporting himself by gambling but aggravating his lung condition along the way. During his travels, he met a prostitute named "Big Nose" Kate Fisher who also went under the name Katie Elder. They became lovers, and according to some reports they were married. The couple settled in Dodge City. Holliday, now known as Doc Holliday, became a friend of Wyatt Earp when he came to his aid during a fracas with some drunken cowhands. The other Earps never liked Holliday—he was, after all, a southerner, and they had all been Unionists—but they tolerated him because of Wyatt.

The trouble in Tombstone came about as a result, one might say, of the civilizing influences that were then taking hold in the West. Older ranching families, who had been living on the frontier since before the Civil War, engaged in practices that later settlers found intolerably lawless. A newspaper founded in the town after the Civil

tures, the Earps had become solid citizens and pillars of the Tombstone community, but there was trouble on the horizon.

When Wyatt Earp left Dodge City for Tombstone, his friend Doc Holliday went with him. John Henry Holliday came from a proper Southern family and was extraordinarily refined—too much so to suit most westerners or even Wyatt's family. He had received a degree in dentistry from the Pennsylvania College of Dental Surgery in

War, the *Tombstone Epitaph*, editorialized against the rowdiness and criminality of one family in particular, that of N.H. "Old Man" Clanton and his three sons, Ike, Phin, and Billy. Between October 1880 and October 1881, a series of incidents inflamed the relationship between the Earps and the Clantons, beginning with the shooting of Marshal Fred White, Wyatt's boss, during an attempt to quiet some Clanton ranch hands. The Earps rounded up some of the Clanton brothers and planned to charge them with the killing, but White admitted before dying that the shooting had been an accident.

In March 1881 a Kinnear and Company stagecoach was held up, and two men were killed. In the minds of the local populace, there was genuine doubt about which camp, the Earps or the Clantons, was responsible; there seemed to be little doubt that it was one of them. At first, public opinion was that Doc Holliday was involved. He was arrested and was about to be charged when he was able to come up with an alibi. The sheriff's office, controlled by the older ranch families, implicated the Earps in the robbery, causing tensions to rise through the summer of 1881. On August 13, Old Man Clanton and some of his hands were shot while rustling cattle in Mexico; rumors spread that they had been killed in their sleep by the Earps.

Wyatt was running for sheriff, so it was important that the stage robbers be apprehended before the election. Wyatt made a deal with Ike Clanton to lead the robbers (who, in truth, were friends of the Clantons and were hiding out on Clanton land) to an ambush in return for several thousand dollars. Ike either double-crossed the robbers or the Earps, but the robbers were found shot in their lair before they could be captured. This made it appear as if the Earps had killed the men who might

have implicated them in the robbery, so Wyatt revealed the details of the deal with Ike, making his feud with the Clantons a blood feud.

On October 26, 1881, the Clantons rode into town to pick up some supplies. They let it be known to the sheriff, John Behan, that they were not looking for a fight with the Earps, though they hated them and had threatened them repeatedly in the previous few days. Behan wanted them to give up their guns, but they refused. Meanwhile, Virgil, now a marshal, deputized Morgan,

James Earp in 1881.

Morgan Earp in 1880.

The O.K. Corral as seen from inside. As an enclosure for town livery, it was surrounded by buildings and not wide open, as it is often depicted.

Wyatt, and Doc Holliday and set out with these deputies to arrest the Clantons. At least that is what they later claimed, but there did not seem to be any charge on which the Clantons could be arrested. The celebrated gunfight between the Earps-Holliday foursome and the Clanton brothers and their allies—Billy Claiborne and the McLaury brothers, Tom and Frank—took place where the Clantons had left their horses, the O.K. Corral, a vacant lot near the livery stable. This gunfight was brief mainly because the Earps and Holliday were the only ones doing the shooting at first. Some of the Clantons, in fact, threw up their hands and surrendered or protested that they were unarmed. When the smoke cleared, the McLaurys were both dead, as was Billy Clanton, although Ike Clanton and Billy Claiborne had managed to run away. On the other side, Virgil and Morgan Earp were wounded, and so was Holliday; Wyatt

was the only participant in the shoot-out left standing.

The aftermath of the shoot-out at the O.K. Corral was tragic: Wyatt Earp and Doc Holliday were tried for murder but the district magistrate, Judge Spicer, dismissed the charges because Earp and Holliday had been deputized and so were carrying out their official duties as officers of the law. Virgil was removed as marshal, and the popularity and fortunes of the Earps began a steep decline. A series of revenge assassination attempts followed, first against Virgil, who survived, and then against Morgan, who was shot in the back while playing pool in a saloon. The Earp clan left the region for California, except for Wyatt and Holliday, who stayed to make certain Morgan's killers were punished. One of the suspected assassins, Frank Stilwell, was found dead, and although Earp had made it clear he was gunning for him, there was no evidence to link him to the crime. Two other suspected accomplices were found shot, and this time there was clear evidence that they had been killed by Wyatt and Holliday. A warrant was issued for their arrest, but it was never served.

Doc Holliday fled to Denver, where he was arrested on trumped-up charges so that he could be extradited to Arizona to stand trial for the murder of Stilwell and his alleged partners. Some of Wyatt's friends, including Bat Masterson, obtained a pardon for Doc Holliday from the governor of Colorado. After that, Holliday drifted, possibly back to Dodge City, got into a series of scrapes with the law, and, with his coughing and lungs getting worse by the day, lived out his last days in a sanitarium in Glenwood Springs, Colorado. He died on November 8, 1887, at the age of thirty-six.

Wyatt moved to California, where he joined Virgil, who lived an interesting life of his own on the West Coast and in Arizona, until he died in 1905 of pneumonia. Of the Earp brothers, Virgil was the one most haunted by Morgan's murder, and several of the gunfights in which he was involved later were connected in some unspecifiable way to the O.K. Corral incident. Wyatt had, in the meantime, married for a third time and spent time in San Francisco and in several other areas of the West seeking his fortune. But fortune never came, and, shortly after he refereed the Bob Fitzsimmons–Tom Sharkey championship boxing match (giving the fight to Sharkey, in what was considered a blatant fix), he went to Alaska and ran a saloon in Nome.

On his return to California in 1901, Wyatt tried, without success, to interest William S. Hart and others in his life story. He acted as a consultant for several films but never was able to make a career of it. It was not until he turned over his notes to biographer Stuart N. Lake that a book was produced.

Lake's *Wyatt Earp: Frontier Marshal* was published in 1931, two years after Earp's death. Lake's biography really opened the floodgates (though Walter Noble Burns began the deluge with his magnificent *Tombstone*, published in 1927).

The Life and Legend of Wyatt Earp, a television series starring Hugh O'Brien, took many liberties with Wyatt's life and mainly advanced the legends. It was the first of the "adult" westerns, in which serious subjects were tackled by the better screenwriters. From 1955 to 1961, it was one of the most popular programs on television and certainly the most popular western of its day—at least in its early days, because the same week it premiered, a totally fictional show premiered. *Gunsmoke* went on to become not only the most popular western but one of the most popular shows in the history of television, airing for some twenty years with the same basic set of characters.

One of the best portrayals of Wyatt Earp on film was also one of the first, although the film was not about Wyatt Earp and did not even have a character by that name. It was the 1932 *Law and Order*, directed by Edward L. Cahn, with Walter Huston as a gunslinging lawman named Saint Johnson, whose life story (in a screenplay by John Huston) was a retelling of the Wyatt Earp story, right down to the gunfight at the O.K. Corral. The film went unappreciated and is now little more than a cult favorite. In 1939 Lake's biography of Earp was adapted to the screen as *Frontier Marshal*, incorporating all of Earp's mistakes and exaggerations. In 1942 Richard Dix gave a memorable portrayal of Wyatt Earp in the little seen *Tombstone, the Town Too Tough to Die*.

The classic portrayal of the Earps and Doc Holliday was in the 1946 John Ford film, *My Darling Clementine*, in which Henry Fonda gave a memorable performance as a contemplatively brazen Wyatt Earp. One might have thought that Ford and Fonda had said it all in 1946, but an even greater classic was John Sturges's *Gunfight at the O.K. Corral*, with Burt Lancaster as Wyatt Earp and Kirk Douglas as Doc Holliday. A film that presents a revisionist (and decidedly unflattering) view of Wyatt Earp and Holliday is Frank Perry's 1971 film, *Doc*, with Stacy Keach in the title role. One of the more interesting films about the period—much more interesting than the lavish but droning 1994 Kevin Costner nonepic—was *I Married Wyatt Earp*, the 1981 film in which Marie Osmond plays Josephine Marcus, the singer from an orthodox Jewish family who became the second Mrs. Wyatt Earp.

The real William Barclay "Bat" Masterson.

BAT MASTERSON

One of the best known of western heroes was William Bartholomew Masterson, better known as Bat Masterson. Masterson changed his name for some unknown reason to William Barclay Masterson, but he continued using the nickname "Bat" throughout his life. He became famous as the dapper lawman who was said to have killed twenty-three men, but he readily admitted that many of the stories that circulated about him (including those he himself spread) were exaggerations.

Bat Masterson was born in 1853 in Quebec, Canada, into a family of seven children. The family moved to New York and then to Illinois before settling in Wichita, Kansas, in 1867. His older brother, Ed, settled in Dodge City in 1872, and Bat moved there to become a buffalo hunter. Bat was in the Battle of Adobe Walls in Texas and fought the Indians led by Quanah Parker. He was later a scout for General Nelson Miles in his campaign against Geronimo.

In 1876 Bat was involved in a gunfight in a saloon in which he killed a man—the only killing for which he was unquestionably responsible. He was enjoying a drink at the bar with a friend, Molly Brennan, when Melvin King, a cavalry soldier and Molly's jealous suitor, entered and shot both her and Masterson. Molly died and Masterson was wounded, but he managed to shoot King and kill him. Masterson was forced to use a cane after that incident, and some believed that was how he got his nickname. The fact is that Bat was a common nickname for Bartholomew, and he was probably called that well before the King shooting.

Masterson moved back to Dodge City in 1877 and became a deputy to his brother Ed, who was the county sheriff. Later in the year, Ed became marshal, and Bat ran for sheriff, winning by three votes. In April of the following year, Ed was involved in a shoot-out with two Texas cowboys, Jack Wagner and Alf Walker, in which he was shot at such close range that his clothes caught on fire. He died a while later, and Bat was said to have avenged his brother's death by summarily shooting the two cowboys dead (although the retaliatory shooting is unconfirmed).

His brother's shooting gave Bat the resolve to become a lawman, and he remained in Dodge City as a marshal. This was a period of vigorous law enforcement and one in which Bat Masterson became famous as an upholder of the law. But he was considered too close to the corrupt mayor and city officials, and in 1879 he was voted out of office.

Bitter and disillusioned, he wandered around the West and finally joined his friends Wyatt Earp and Luke Short in Tombstone in 1881. Later in the year, Bat received a call for help from his brother Jim. Jim was having trouble in Dodge City with his two partners in the saloon he ran, the Lady Gay Dance Hall and Saloon. On April 16, Bat got off the train at Dodge City and began shooting almost instantly. One of the partners, Al Updegraff, was shot down, and the other partner, A.J. Peacock, took off when the mayor and the sheriff intervened. Bat was given a token fine and, within hours of arriving, was on the train on his way back to Tombstone.

Bat soon settled in Denver, but he traveled across the West, making a good living at the gambling tables and as part-time manager of the Palace Theater in Denver. Several times in the late 1880s he came to the aid of fellow gamblers Doc Holliday and Luke Short. In 1891 he married Emma Walters, and the city officials of Denver hoped he would settle down. But the fact that he spent more time in Denver because of Emma turned out to be a problem because, as was the case with many gamblers, he had to be proficient with a gun to protect himself from sore losers or card players who attributed his luck to cheating.

In the decade that followed, Bat Masterson seemed to live two very different lives (probably depending on the influence of two people—Emma and Luke Short). He drank heavily, and then he became a prohibitionist and helped close down the saloon in Dodge City. At one point, he joined an anti-gambling crusade, and at another, he opened a gambling hall with Short in Fort Worth, Texas. As gambling became a disreputable occupation in the West, Masterson tried to clean up his act and become associated with the more respectable gambling houses in Texas. But by 1902, a "respectable gambling house" was an oxymoron, and in that year, Bat Masterson simply turned his back on the West and moved to New York City.

Gene Barry as Bat Masterson in the TV series Gunsmoke.

In New York, he was appointed marshal, as a ceremonial position, by President Theodore Roosevelt, but he was later removed by President Taft. Masterson moved in high social circles and was the subject of articles and a novel by journalist Alfred Henry Lewis. He had tried his hand at newspaper publishing in Denver just briefly, and, when money got tight for the Mastersons, Bat wrote a series of articles called "Famous Gun Fighters of the Western Frontier." Through this series, eastern readers became more familiar with legends like Wyatt Earp, Doc Holliday, Ben Thompson, Luke Short, Bill Tilgham, and Buffalo Bill Cody—and, of course, Bat Masterson himself. The articles looked at the art of gunfighting almost clinically. He taught, for example, that a gunfighter ought to aim at the widest portion of the body, the midsection, and not the head, as gun duelers often did; Bat claimed to have trained many future Texas Rangers.

Having promoted several boxing matches in Denver and fancying himself an expert on boxing, he became a sports editor of the *Morning Telegraph* and covered the sports beat competently. Bat said he hated being constantly reminded of his days in the Old West, yet he often purchased old guns in pawnshops, cleaned them up and inscribed them, and then gave them out as souvenirs, claiming he had used them in one gunfight or another. He died of a heart attack at his desk at the *Morning Telegraph* (in the middle of writing his column) on October 25, 1921.

In 1957 a biography about Masterson by Richard O'Connor appeared that relied heavily on Masterson's own articles. Much of the biography was simply exaggeration. More reliable sources are a 1960 work by Z.A. Tilghman, *Spotlight: Bat Masterson and Wyatt Earp as Deputy U.S. Marshals,* and George Thompson's 1943 work, *Bat Masterson: The Dodge City Years.* Thompson's work was heavily relied on in creating the television series *Bat Masterson,* starring Gene Barry, a program that aired between 1958 and 1961. Barry's Masterson may have been a bit more polished than the genuine article, but the real Masterson did wear derby hats and sport silver-tipped canes and special, snub-nosed guns that fit neatly into a belt under his jacket.

Because of his association with the likes of Wyatt Earp and Luke Short, Masterson appeared in a number of films about other western legends or about the famous shoot-out at the O.K. Corral. Several movies were made that focus on his life, however, with Masterson played by actors such as Randolph Scott and Joel McCrea. One film stands out from the rest because it deals with the conflict he felt about Emma, the urge to gamble, and his interest in following in his brother's footsteps as a lawman. This is the 1943 film *Woman of the Town,* starring Albert Dekker as a Masterson with some dimension, whose love interest is killed during a shoot-out with the criminal element of the town.

THE THREE OKLAHOMA GUARDSMEN

The Three Guardsmen of Oklahoma were lawmen at the turn of the century who helped to tame one of the roughest areas—the Indian Territory of Oklahoma. Their names—Heck Thomas, Bill Tilgham, and Christian Madsen—became famous during their lifetimes, partly because of the increased abilities of newspapers to cover and report stories through-out the country. Fifty years earlier, the same lawmen would probably have had to rely on later chroniclers to spread their fame.

The other distinguishing feature of these men was that there was never any doubt as to which side of the law they were on. Unlike other heroes, their hats were always white, and usually the purest shade of white. This is not to say they were not violent. A violent, almost trigger-happy temperament was one of the items in the lawman's arsenal that kept him alive; very rarely was a lawman of the West chastised for acting too quickly or too harshly in dealing with any situation. But for the most part these three acted within the bounds of the law and were all that stood between the ordinary citizen and the victimizing bandits and outlaws of the period.

Henry Andrew "Heck" Thomas was born in Oxford, Georgia, in 1850. He fought for the Confederacy under Stonewall Jackson during the Civil War. Almost immediately after the war, he went into law enforcement, first as a policeman in Georgia, and then as a guard and agent for the Texas Express Company, a shipping arm of the Houston and Texas Central Railway Company. He almost immediately became famous for foiling a robbery attempt by the Sam Bass gang on March 18, 1878. Having a strong hunch that the gang was going to rob the train, he hid the twenty-five thousand dollars he was carrying in the freight car's stove and substituted wads of paper and a few cover bills and money binders in the burlap money bags in the freight car's safe. To make the switch a bit more believable, he attempted to stop the robbers and was wounded; the gang made off with eighty-nine dollars in cash. Thomas spent the next two years recovering from his wounds (and basking in his newfound glory). He became a deputy of the Western District of Arkansas in 1881

Bill Tilgham, Oklahoma City Chief of Police, in 1912.

U.S. Deputy Marshal Heck Thomas.

Chris Madsen, Oklahoma City Deputy, photographed in 1937 at a convention of the National Frontiersmen's Association, Houston.

and then went to work for Judge Isaac Parker, the "Hanging Judge" of Fort Smith. The Thomas-Parker team cleared the area with deadly efficiency, bringing many outlaws to justice, many of them sentenced to hanging by Parker.

Thomas was responsible for ending the criminal careers of several of the most violent outlaws of the Oklahoma panhandle area. When the Oklahoma Territory that had been occupied by the Indians was opened to white settlers and several "runs" for land took place, Oklahoma suddenly found itself to be an area on the wild frontier and in a more primitive, lawless state than settled areas well to the west. It was as if the Old West had been reinvented, and the lawmen who brought order to the area, no less than the gamblers, saloon keepers, and bandits, found a new theater of operation. The Three Guardsmen operated for the most part independently and each cleared out a different lawless element of the area, but together they made Oklahoma a viable civilized area, which led directly to its becoming a state in 1907.

Thomas was responsible for bringing to justice the Doolin, Buck, and Dalton gangs,

as well as bringing in the Cherokee outlaw Ned Christie. A case that was followed carefully was his capture of Jim July—the bandit accused of murdering Belle Starr—who died in prison awaiting trial. Thomas remained a law enforcer in Lawton, Oklahoma, until 1909, when age finally caught up with him. He retired and lived in Lawton until he died in his sleep on August 11, 1912, at the age of sixty-two.

The second of the Three Guardsmen was a man who teamed up with Heck Thomas on occasion: Bill Tilghman. Tilghman (pronounced *Till-man*) was one of the most celebrated lawmen of the West and was active as a marshal right up to his death. William Mathew Tilghman was born in Iowa in 1854. As a young man, he was Bat Masterson's deputy when Masterson was marshal of Dodge City in 1878. Tilghman later became marshal and served there until 1889, when he joined the land run into Indian Territory in what was to become Oklahoma, settling in Guthrie, a boomtown in the Oklahoma Panhandle.

Tilghman first achieved notoriety in Oklahoma by capturing two women outlaws—Jennie "Little Britches" Stevens and Cattle Annie McDougal—in 1894. He rose through the ranks of Oklahoma lawmen, serving as the chief of police in Oklahoma City from 1911 to 1924. He also made several trips to California during this period and became a friend and advisor to William S. Hart, who called him "Uncle Billy" Tilghman. Tilghman did not care for the name, but he did supervise the production of a movie, *The Passing of the Oklahoma Outlaws*, which was released in 1915.

After retiring, Tilghman settled in Cromwell, Oklahoma, and became the town marshal, a position he filled vigorously and not merely symbolically. On November 1, 1924, he was in the process of taking in a rowdy and drunken Prohibition agent

In spite of the chaos the land rushes created, the cavalry maintained some semblance of order when it came to safeguarding claims or preventing settlers from staking a claim too early. In this illustration, the cavalry is escorting a family of boomers out of Oklahoma Territory, probably because they "rushed" too soon.

named Wiley Lynn. On their way to jail, Lynn took out a small pistol from under his clothing and shot Tilghman in the chest, killing him. Lynn surrendered to the authorities, and was tried, but was, amazingly, acquitted. The entire Oklahoma law enforcement community came down on Lynn, and he was harassed until 1932, when an Oklahoma state officer, Crockett Long, goaded him into a fight and killed him.

The third Guardsman, Christian "Chris" Madsen, was born in Copenhagen in 1851 and did not arrive in the United States until 1871 (or, according to some sources, in 1876). Before reaching America, he had fought with the French Foreign Legion in the Franco-Prussian War and had been at the Battle of Sedan, so naturally he joined the U.S. Army, becoming a member of the Fifth Cavalry. He fought with the U.S. Army in some of the major engagements of the Indian Wars and was present (he claimed) when Buffalo Bill Cody killed Chief Yellow Hand at War Bonnet Creek. By 1891 Madsen was married with a family and, having tried unsuccessfully to start a farm, was hired as a deputy U.S. marshal by Marshal William Grimes. (Tilghman and Thomas had started out the same way and may have served with Madsen as deputies at the same time.)

It was in the period between 1891 and 1898 that Madsen did most of the outlaw-clearing work that made him the Third Guardsman. He left law enforcement for a period, and after his wife died in 1899, he rode with Teddy Roosevelt's Rough Riders in Cuba. He was appointed marshal of Oklahoma in 1911. By then, the state was fully under the jurisdiction of the federal government and Madsen—and other old-timers—had become superfluous. He retired for good in 1922 and settled down in Guthrie. A bout of yellow jack fever contracted in Cuba plagued him throughout

his old age, but he managed to live to the age of ninety-three, dying on January 9, 1944 (although some believe he died in 1948).

Because the Three Guardsmen operated relatively late in the game, significantly better records and more documentation exist for them than for other western figures. As a result, there have been several excellent books on the lives of these three lawmen and on the period: Homer Croy's *Trigger Marshal* (1958) is a thrilling biography of Chris Madsen (whose life also seems to be the stuff great movies are made of); Heck Thomas's life is reviewed in glorious and accurate detail in Glenn Shirley's 1962 biography of him; and two works on Bill Tilgham—one by his daughter (1944) and the other by F. Miller (1967)—admirably portray him as the "last frontier marshal." The 1929 work by Hines and Nix on the

The Oklahoma Land Rush of 1889 sent thousands of new settlers into the area in a short time, creating many problems in maintaining order.

Oklahombres beautifully evokes the wild and lawless atmosphere of the times.

The problem with many of these works is that they do not realize that the Oklahoma of the turn of the century was not really the Old West but a recreation of it in microcosm, a product of several accidents of American history. This is the reason several important histories of the American West and reference books on the subject do not regard the period or the Three Guardsmen as subjects of western American history. The methods and environment of Oklahoma were throwbacks to the Old West, but a number of things had changed. For one thing, the war with the Indians was over. The lack of an Indian threat from the unknown frontier made a huge difference in the lives of the people. It was also the case that, instead of radiating *out* to a wilderness and setting down new and unrepressed roots, the area encircling Oklahoma poured settlers *into* it, bringing with them the civility and conventions of settled areas. And the question of incorporation of new lands into the United States, which was the key issue in the nineteenth century, was all but settled now.

The Oklahomans found themselves with the appearances of the Old West but without its context, like children donning western outfits and playing Wild West games. In fact, many of the images that come to us from Oklahoma at that time appear to be almost like easterners wearing costumes for the camera as tourists might. The problems the Three Guardsmen faced were very similar to those faced in the Old West, and the methods they and their adversaries used were akin to those found in the West of fifty years before—which is why they are included in this work. But there is a great deal of difference between a lawman fighting a desperado with little or no hope of being helped or rescued by the U.S. cavalry,

and one fighting an outlaw surrounded by a nation, with its entire legal and military apparatus all about and at the ready.

THE TEXAS RANGERS

A section on the Texas Rangers is included because of the role this group has played in getting Americans interested in the Old West. Like many Americans who grew up in the 1950s, the television program *The Lone Ranger* had a mesmerizing effect on me and sent me scurrying to the library. Fortunately, my local public library was large enough to have a worn, rebound copy of Walter Prescott Webb's 1934 book about the Texas Rangers, long out of print and not widely available (until it was reprinted in 1965). The program actually had a special meaning to me for the simple reason that my Brooklyn neighborhood looked very much like the ramshackle streets of the towns of most of the television westerns—although the wide-open spaces that were the backdrop for *The Lone Ranger* were completely different. When it became clear that the Lone Ranger was not remotely typical of the West, that it was mythology in the classic sense—incorporating an ethos and a consciousness of one era looking at another— I began a long journey to understand the West in as realistic terms as possible.

The Texas Rangers were a gift that Stephen Austin bequeathed to Texas when he created a band of men who would protect settlers from attacks by Indians while the main armed force was directed southward against the Mexicans. The rangers were officially sanctioned in 1835, but they

Frank Hamer (bottom, right) is usually depicted as tracking, and then shooting, Bonnie and Clyde by himself. While he was indeed a Special Officer of the Texas Rangers assigned to the case, he was assisted by the law enforcement officers pictured here.

were functioning unofficially as early as 1826. When relations with the Mexicans deteriorated, the rangers, now organized as a band of mounted, uniformed soldiers but lacking many of the standard elements of a military force or state militia (no surgeon, no flag, no standard-issue arms, or even horses), also protected the settlers from the Mexicans. In the Mexican War, units of Texas Rangers fought under generals Zachary Taylor and Winfield Scott, and they continued to guard against Mexican incursion even after Texas was admitted into the Union in 1845.

After the Civil War, the rangers turned their attention to eradicating from the Texas frontier the lawless gangs and outlaws that preyed on the settlers who were trying to establish ranches and farms. And, in fact, many of the outlaws who terrorized Texas were brought to justice by the rangers. In 1874 the rangers were divided into two main battalions: one, the Frontier Battalion, concentrated on containing the Indians; the other, the Special Forces, concentrated on eliminating rustling and robbery, especially along the Mexican border. Their total number rarely exceeded one hundred; the

rangers preferred a small elite force to large numbers. In a sense, then, every Texas Ranger was, in some way, "Lone."

The rangers did not disband in the twentieth century even when the last outlaws on their "wanted" list, Bonnie Parker and Clyde Barrow, were killed by Ranger Frank Hamer in 1934, and their original mission no longer remained. They became part of the Texas Department of Public Safety in 1935 and were a small, virtually independent force fighting on behalf of law and order in the state and operating under the authority of the state government. (This arrangement, unusual in police circles, has sometimes created opportunities for abuse, particularly in terms of the treatment of anyone other than white Anglo-Saxon males. Some gubernatorial candidates have even run on platforms calling for disbanding the rangers, but the group has continued to demonstrate its usefulness and has tried to broaden its roster and sensitize its officers to serve the widest constituency possible; it is not an easy task.)

In the period before the Civil War, a number of Texas Rangers became celebrated in American lore. One of the earliest rangers,

The photo (above) for which the real Bonnie Parker and Clyde Barrow posed (and which they sent to the newspapers) was recreated (right) by Faye Dunaway and Warren Beatty in the 1967 film Bonnie and Clyde.

and one of the best, was Jesse Lee "Red" Hall, a native of North Carolina who, as a ranger, arrested the notorious outlaw John King Fisher. Hall's most important contribution, however, was in quelling the infamous Sutton-Taylor feud, which had begun in the Carolinas and spilled from state to state, involving hundreds of combatants and resulting in the deaths of scores of innocent people on both sides. Hall finally brought peace to De Witt County, where the feud raged, in 1875. He died in San Antonio in

1911 after serving as an Indian agent and in the Philippines during the Spanish-American War.

One of the keys to the rangers' success was their use of the latest revolvers manufactured by the Colt Company, especially the Colt .45. Their exclusive use of Colt guns made the small ranger force formidable, especially against Indians and Mexicans, who were accustomed to fighting Texans who were using single-shot weapons. The use of the Colt weapons was the brainchild of John Coffee Hays, a Tennesseean who became a captain of the rangers in 1840 at the young age of twenty-three. He led them to victories over much larger numbers of Comanches, such as at the Battle of Bandera Pass in 1841. Hays also instilled in the rangers a brazen attitude, and had them habitually charge into the enemy lines instead of taking up a defensive position, which became a part of the ranger approach to crime-fighting. After Texas statehood, Hays anticipated that the rangers would be disbanded, so he moved to California and became sheriff of San Francisco County.

One of the rangers under Hays's command was a huge Virginian named William Alexander Wallace, who went by the name "Bigfoot" Wallace. Wallace was over six feet tall (his shoe size is not known), and with his scraggly beard he must have presented quite a sight to any Indians or outlaws he was fighting. Wallace eventually came to command his own ranger company, but he is best remembered for several tall tales he donated to American folklore, especially one in which he took on a mob of Indians protected by a suit of armor he made out of hickory nut shells.

Rangers prided themselves on having excellent tracking abilities, particularly in the Texas underbrush, a difficult place to track anything. This tradition was the legacy of John Reynolds Hughes, an Illinois native who lived with the Indians in Oklahoma, where he learned the fine art of tracking. This training came in handy when he tracked horse rustlers who had taken his herd across twelve hundred miles (1,920km) of the Texas wilderness, finally catching up with the gang and arresting them. After serving in the rangers for twenty-eight years, Hughes retired in 1915. He became a bank president in El Paso, and died in 1947 at age ninety-two. The training program set up by Hughes and improved on continually over the years (including introducing state-of-the-art technology to the problem of finding people) has made the rangers a valuable resource in finding escaped criminals or tracking down anyone lost or wanted by the law.

After the Civil War, with Texas firmly a part of the United States, a new crop of ranger leaders brought the group forward. The man most responsible for the rejuvenation of the institution of the Texas Rangers was Leander H. McNelly, a frail and soft-spoken Texan who recruited the best men he could find. It was during McNelly's tenure as commander that integrity and incorruptibility became part of what it meant to wear the ranger badge. McNelly's lieutenant, a robust ranger named John Barclay Armstrong, did much of the arduous work involved in field command, including tracking and bringing in John Wesley Hardin to stand trial. Armstrong became known as "McNelly's Bulldog."

McNelly's most ambitious and most controversial ranger action was the pursuit of the Mexican bandit Juan Cortinas into Mexico. Slowly, the rangers secured the border areas and towns so that the Cortinistas were severely restricted in how deeply they could go across the Rio Grande on their marauding raids. In 1875 McNelly decided it was time to put a stop to Cortinas once and for all, and the Special Forces battalion of the rangers crossed the border and went after the Mexican bandits. The Mexicans were more familiar with the terrain, however, and McNelly's men soon found themselves pinned down and surrounded. American troops had been following ranger progress from the northern side of the border, and when they feared the rangers would be massacred, they crossed into Mexico and drove the Cortinistas away. When the army commander insisted that McNelly return to American soil, McNelly reportedly told him to convey his compliments to the secretary of war, but the rangers would not leave until they were good and ready. The experience taught the U.S. government to intervene early with the U.S. Cavalry in dealing with the raids of Pancho Villa's revolutionaries in 1916 and not to allow the rangers to face Villa's army of ten thousand with their hundred or so men.

Toward the end of his life—he died in 1877—McNelly was so sick that he directed the rangers from a bed in a wagon. After he died, Red Hall took over his command. Meanwhile, Armstrong lived to 1913, dying peacefully on his Willacy County ranch at age sixty-three.

The Texas Rangers became celebrated in the 1860s with "The Texas Rangers," one of the most popular and enduring of cowboy songs. The rangers were a constant source of legends and news, possibly because they represented a law enforcement group that still championed the abilities of the individual in an era when specialists and teams made up most police departments.

Webb's book, *The Texas Rangers*, collected much valuable information and cleared up much of the confusion. Biographies of individual rangers often shed light on the times and the institution: Stanley Vestal wrote a fascinating biography of Bigfoot Wallace, and E. Cunningham's *Triggernometry: A Gallery of Gunfighters*, published in 1934, looks at the careers of rangers and the outlaws they bested. A book that had a wide influence and conveyed a sense of the training and commitment of the rangers was J.B. Gillett's 1921 work, *Six Years with the Texas Rangers, 1875–1881*.

The rangers have been amply portrayed in film and on television over the century but usually in clichéd terms or in very superficial portrayals. Tom Mix played a Texas Ranger in the classic 1921 film *Riders*

of the Purple Sage, and some critics point to that film as one of the best of the western genre. A 1936 King Vidor production, *The Texas Rangers*, which, as was often the case, benefited from the advice of William S. Hart, was probably the most polished of the pre–World War II films about the rangers. Meanwhile, *The Lone Ranger* radio program, created by George Trendle (who was also in charge of the television series), and the Republic "B" serials enthralled youngsters throughout the 1920s and 1930s. In the earliest days of commercial television, the Lone Ranger was looked upon as a character that would certainly be made into a program once there were enough sets in American homes.

After the war, with the boom in westerns in movie theaters and on the TV screen, the Texas Rangers appeared in a number of routine films—including the 1949 *Streets of Laredo*, based on the Vidor film, as well as a pale 1951 remake of the Vidor film with the same title. Meanwhile, *The Lone Ranger* was beginning to establish itself as a television staple. Clayton Moore starred during all but two of the seasons the show ran—1949 to 1954. The program presented the basic story in the first episode: a Texas Ranger named John Reid is one of six rangers ambushed by the Butch Cavendish Gang. During the attack, the others are killed, but Reid is left for dead and is found by an Indian, Tonto, played throughout the series by Jay Silverheels. Tonto nurses him back to health, and Reid buries the other rangers, creating a sixth grave to fool the Cavendish Gang into believing they killed all six rangers. He begins life anew as the Lone Ranger, a masked rider who fights injustice wherever he finds it while on his way to his real goal, which is to bring the Cavendish Gang to justice. The squeaky clean image of the Lone Ranger—he never drinks, smokes, or curses; he never seems

Occasionally, Texas Rangers had to raid an entire town when the criminal element was too powerful to be handled by local law enforcement, as when they swept through the town of Kilgore, Texas, arresting scores of miscreants and holding them in the local Baptist church.

to have any love life; and he never shoots to kill, only to maim or to disarm—was, of course, a myth. But it was one that writers and filmmakers could use as a device with which to mirror social issues and human qualities, good and bad (which is, after all, the ultimate purpose of a myth).

In the 1960s, Hollywood tried to develop the image of the Texas Rangers along more human and humorous lines in films like the 1968 film *Three Guns for Texas*, which became the basis for the television series *Laredo*, an hour-long western that presented three Texas Rangers in a lighthearted (though not comic) light. This contrasted radically with the austere image presented in the program *Tales of the Texas Rangers*, a television version of the radio program that had starred Joel McCrea and that had in it the seed of the "cop reality" shows which have become popular in the 1980s and 1990s. Two films that took a more serious and complex look at the Texas Rangers were the 1956 *The Searchers*, a John Ford classic (regarded by some as the model western), with John Wayne as a ranger tracking his niece who has been kidnapped by Indians, and *The Comancheros*, a 1961 film also starring Wayne, this time as a ranger who infiltrates a gang of gunrunners to the Indians, which was directed by Michael Curtiz (his last film). Both films relied heavily on the special abilities developed in the training of the Texas Rangers and on their personal code of honor—in *The Searchers* to paradoxical effect when the protagonist is discovered to be also intent on killing his niece for having been "defiled" by the Indians.

In the 1980s, the Texas Rangers were seen as having something in common with martial arts films, in which single warriors defeat scores of enemies in comic ballet. Chuck Norris thus found the portrayal of a kick-boxing Texas Ranger ideally suited to his acting style in the 1983 film *Lone Wolf*

Clayton Moore as the Lone Ranger with his horse, Silver, at the height of the popularity of the 1950s television series The Lone Ranger.

McQuade and later reprised the type in the successful television series *Walker, Texas Ranger*.

The efforts to update the Lone Ranger legend have not fared as well. The 1981 film *The Legend of the Lone Ranger* was flat and uninteresting, precisely because it avoided the elements that are crucial to legend—such elements as the suspension of disbelief, the personalization of values in characters, and the stark and bold relief in which characters are portrayed. It was, in other words, a rendering in which every element of mystery and fantasy had been distilled out, making the Lone Ranger (played by Klinton Spillsbury, but with his voice terribly dubbed) little more than a cowboy who needed to get out more.

Critics thought the failure of the Lone Ranger film in the 1980s was evidence that the age of legend-making was over. But the popularity of science fiction films like the Star Wars trilogy and the successful film realizations of cartoon legends from Batman and Dick Tracy to the Flintstones demonstrate that the public's appetite for legend has not been sated—indicating that another attempt at the Lone Ranger may not be long in coming.

CAVALRY CAPS

The Soldiers

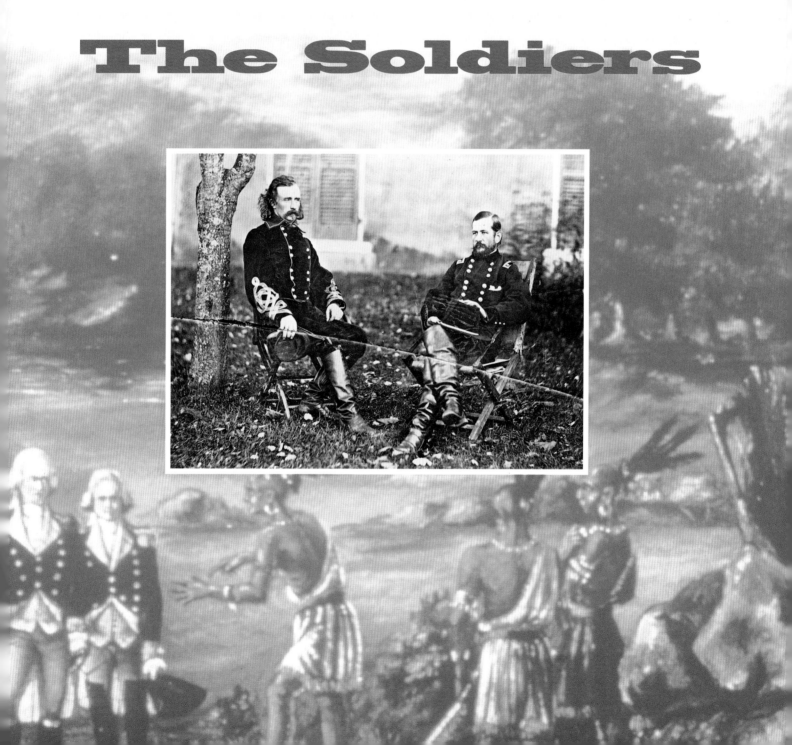

The issue of the Indians on the North American continent was pressing since colonial times, and the Revolutionary War only confused the issue further. The Indians were nearly always successfully recruited by the British and remained in conflict with the colonists even after the Treaty of Paris, to which they were not a party, was signed in 1783. Having to choose between, on the one hand, a distant king, allegiance to whom they could understand as consistent with their own social structure, and, on the other hand, the colonists, with whom they were in close proximity and dealt on a daily basis, was difficult enough. But then they encountered another authority: a remote and faceless body of men called "Congress," who in some way represented the interests of the local regions (a concept not unfamiliar to the Indians, who sometimes convened councils of elders to settle intertribal disputes), but in other ways exercised control over the regions with, it seemed, near-absolute authority. The Indians were not in a position to recognize or comprehend the power struggle that would ensue between

the states, Congress, and the president, only to be resolved in a bloody Civil War. (More cultivated European nations found American politics no less vexing.) Neither did they regard themselves as a conquered people simply because their erstwhile allies, the British, lost the war.

From 1783 to the end of the Civil War, a policy emerged that placed the U.S. Army in the pivotal roles of carrying out U.S. policy toward the Indians and directing U.S. activities in the West through the latter half of the nineteenth century. That policy toward the Indians consisted of the following elements: first, Congress asserted its authority to deal with the Indians as an extension of the Articles of Confederation and in Congress's treaty-affirming powers. Then, Congress asserted authority over the setting of boundary lines between Indian lands and those of the United States, an extension of the policy set forth in the Proclamation of 1763. These two guiding principles proved difficult to carry out, partly because the Indians saw no reason to accept Congress's belief that a treaty was required by which lands would be exchanged for peace, but mainly because the settlers (not very much more expert at the mechanisms of their newly created government than the Indians) saw no reason to refrain from encroaching on lands beyond the borders delineated in those treaties. Without an armed force to intimidate the Indians and control white encroachment, Congress had little choice but to renegotiate the treaties each time their violation became intolerable. Little wonder, then, that early in the game, Indians lost faith in the will or ability of Congress to keep its word and uphold its own treaties.

The war that followed demonstrated two things. First, battle against the Indians was going to be no easy matter; after a series of defeats, Washington's secretary of war, Henry Knox, called upon General "Mad" Anthony Wayne, who triumphed over the Indians at the Battle of Fallen Timbers. When the British, who had encouraged the Indians, suddenly abandoned them, the Indians sued for peace and accepted the terms of the Treaty of Greenville, which ceded Ohio and Indiana to the United States. Thus began a retreat that was to push them across the continent.

Second, the early confrontations showed that the settlers had a decided advantage because of the way they occupied the land.

Above: A decisive turning point in the war against the Indians came in 1794 when Mad Anthony Wayne led American troops to victory at the Battle of Fallen Timbers. Opposite: General George Armstrong Custer, celebrated at the time of this portrait as the "Boy General."

While the Indians generally attempted to form self-contained systems that allowed them to move across the landscape and take advantage of the wide-open spaces, white settlers dug their roots deep and relied on commercial connections with other communities to respond to inevitable momentary shortfalls in crops and supplies. It was a system that they had brought over from Europe and that had its roots in the medieval adaptation of systems developed by the Roman Empire. We may take it for granted today, but anthropologists have become acutely aware of how particular European settling practices are and how they both provided advantages and incurred costs to the settlers.

In the early nineteenth century, there were periods when the federal government sought to "civilize" the Indians by funding educational and missionary projects. But the major policy was one of removal. President Jackson was particularly insistent on pursuing a policy of removal, and by the mid-1830s, either by treaty or by military action, Indians had been resettled west of the Mississippi. Much of this land, of course, already belonged to the United States, and it was clear that the problem would recur when the push westward

brought white Americans once again into contact and conflict with the Indians. The transfer of responsibility of dealing with the Indians from the War Department to the newly formed Department of the Interior may have signaled a change in federal intentions to those who argued (there were, sad to say, not many) throughout the century that the issue was not a military one.

After the Civil War, the U.S. Army was greatly reduced, and many generals were recommissioned at lower rank, because there simply was no need for so many commanders. These generals of the North did not, as a rule, enjoy the benefits of victory—that was reserved for the politicians. After more than a century of war—against Spain, France, England (twice), Mexico, the Indians, and finally, each other, in the War Between the States—the military was not inclined simply to fade away just because America had run out of enemies. Settlement of the West was stepping up and that would inevitably lead to confrontations with the Indians, an adversary the army felt confident fighting. The fact that two presidents, Harrison and Jackson, had been elected before the Civil War largely because of their heroics in fighting Indians did not escape the attention of these generals or their even more ambitious junior officers.

The period from 1865 to 1891, then, became the period of the Indian Wars of the West. This war was carried out by the U.S. Army, sometimes at the behest of the federal government, sometimes at the behest of the local authorities, and sometimes without any more authorization than the personal predilections of field commanders. Sometimes the federal authorities, from the president on down, looked the other way when the army acted on its own or contrary to stated U.S. government policy, because rarely did the outcome displease. When outrage was expressed against any military commander for overstepping his authority or committing some atrocity, disciplinary action was considered in the context of not wishing to discourage this sort of military initiative on the whole.

The soldiers whose stories appear below were heroes in their day, and were often the recipients of medals and gifts of gratitude from settlers and admirers even after being reprimanded by officialdom. Making western territories fit for statehood was a direct and palpable consequence of the army's actions, and these constituencies realized their debt to the U.S. Cavalry. In this period, America came to take for itself the prerogative of deciding who its heroes and villains were—a tradition that has become a permanent feature of American culture and that has confounded the rest of the world ever since.

GEORGE ARMSTRONG CUSTER

Few individuals in American history have experienced such a reversal of fortune and reputation as has General George Armstrong Custer. For a century, the defeat of the Seventh Cavalry at the Battle of the Little Big Horn was regarded as a tragic moment in American history, and the massacre was used as a justification for the ongoing war against the Indians. "General" Custer was actually a lieutenant colonel, but because he had been a general in the Civil War, it was customary to continue calling him general afterward. He was seen as a martyr to the cause of Manifest Destiny; Sitting Bull, the

leader of the combined forces of the Sioux and Cheyenne tribes, was seen as the personification of the evil savage that the U.S. Army had every right to destroy and remove from the land.

In the last twenty-five years, a different attitude has taken hold. Whether or not the Americans of European stock who ventured

more shameful episodes in American history. In the shift of historical perspective, Custer went from martyr to villain, and under scrutiny, it came to seem amazing that he was ever admired or given a position of any responsibility.

George Armstrong Custer was born into a prominent family of Hessian ancestry in

Custer's Last Stand, a popular subject for artists, was probably not as orderly a military operation as depicted here.

out into the West, or the government that represented them back east, had many alternatives is debatable. But it is now understood that the policy that was actually carried out drew on the most base instincts of humanity and amounted to nothing less than the genocidal displacement of an entire race of people. There is little doubt that the policy of incorporating the western lands into the United States and ridding them of its native peoples was one of the

Rumley, Ohio, on December 5, 1839, the first of five children. Custer was not a very good student, but as the eldest son of a prominent family, he was appointed to the U.S. Military Academy at West Point. He graduated at the very bottom of his class and frequently had to be disciplined. After graduation, Custer was assigned to the Fifth Cavalry of the Army of the Potomac, where he soon impressed generals George McClellan and Phil Kearny with his almost reckless courage and bravado. In 1863 Custer was promoted to the rank of brigadier general (although it later appeared that the promotion had been the result of a clerical error).

Custer was a great believer in the power of the element of surprise and took great pains to hide his whereabouts from his adversaries. Unfortunately, this also meant that he was loathe to send out scouts for fear they would betray his presence, so he often attacked his enemies knowing as little about them as they knew about his forces. As long as the Fifth Cavalry was numerically superior, Custer could get away with this, and indeed he early gained a reputation for being a very able and resourceful (and, perhaps more importantly, lucky) commander.

During the Civil War, he was credited with leading the cavalry charge that prevented Jeb Stuart from outflanking the Union Army at Gettysburg, and he was one of the heroes at the Battle of Bull Run. After the war, General Grant presented to Custer a gift of the table in the Appomattox courthouse on which Lee had signed the terms of surrender. When the army was reorganized, Custer was made a lieutenant colonel and was put in command of the Seventh Cavalry; their orders were to maintain order and keep the Indians in the western territories under control.

A vain man, Custer wore his blond hair long, partly to give him a more youthful appearance—he delighted in being known as the "boy general"—and partly to show his contempt for the Indian custom of scalping dead victims as trophies of battle. He was also a pompous man who believed in the strictest discipline, which often entailed harsh punishment for even the slightest of infractions, and in whipping his soldiers into shape through the most severe maneuvers and long periods of pointless marching. Custer's disciplining of

his soldiers resulted in his being court-martialed in 1867 and found guilty. This might have meant the end of Custer's career, but General Sheridan had a special assignment for him and Custer was reinstated.

The assignment was to lead the Seventh Cavalry in a winter campaign against the Arapaho and the Cheyenne in an effort to force them onto a reservation near Fort Cobb, where they would find it difficult to stage their customary summer raids. The Seventh was sent out from Camp Supply, Oklahoma, under Custer's command, with the intent of attacking the Cheyenne villages outside the designated reservation. The troop soon found itself in a snowstorm, and when an Indian village appeared on the banks of the Washita in the distance in front of the column, Custer organized a four-pronged attack. On the morning of November 17, 1868, with the band playing the regiment's battle song, "Carryowen," the village was surrounded. Many of the inhabitants were killed (including the chief, Black Kettle), and the area was secured. It turned out, however, to be the wrong village. It was already on the reservation, a peaceful village that had been guaranteed safety from assault by the commander at Camp Supply. None of this concerned Custer, however, and the Battle of Washita became a celebrated episode in Custer's Indian-fighting career.

During the battle, Indian warriors in other villages along the Washita were alerted and came to the defense of Black Kettle. Custer fought them off and then retreated, abandoning a squadron of nineteen men he had sent on ahead. When the men were later found dead, the incident became a focus of great distrust of Custer on the part of his men.

Custer had married in 1864—his wife was Elizabeth "Libbie" Bacon, daughter of a wealthy family that was influential in

Custer's last moments at the Battle of the Little Big Horn.

A Native American version of the Battle of the Little Big Horn, drawn by tribal scribe White Bird.

office. With the support of people such as James Gordon Bennett, publisher of the *New York Herald*, such an ambition was certainly not out of the question. (Custer's marriage did not prevent him from taking Monahseetaha, a comely Indian girl who survived the Battle of Washita, and making her his live-in interpreter, though she did not speak a word of English.)

Custer had gained a reputation as a fearless cavalry officer in the war and a great Indian fighter at the Washita—a reputation that owed much to the slanted accounts of *Herald* reporter Randolph Keim and Custer's own book (written largely by Libbie), titled *My Life on the Plains*. Yet he needed to do two things if he was to ever mount a campaign for the presidency: distance himself from the scandal-ridden Grant administration and become the man who, once and for all, put an end to the Indian menace in the West. The problem was that these two goals were contrary to one another because President Grant

Michigan politics. On several occasions, Custer marched his entire regiment home when he received word that his wife was ill. (Interestingly, one of the charges brought in the 1867 court-martial was that Custer had had soldiers shot who left to visit sick wives.) The couple were much sought after in Washington and New York, and both certainly had high political aspirations, possibly to the White House after Grant's term of

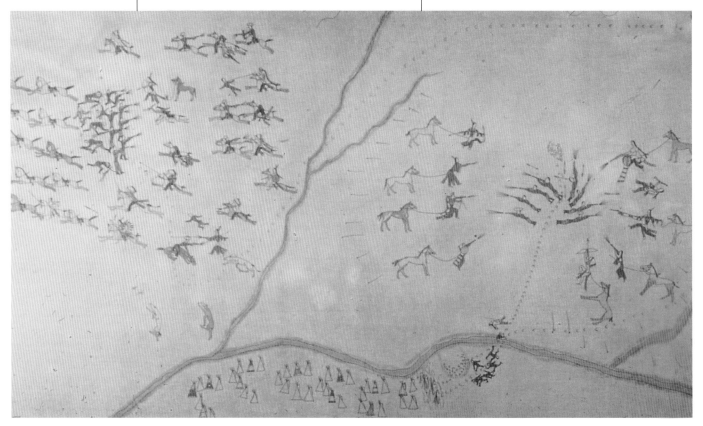

decided for himself who was going to command the regiments of the army. When Custer testified against Secretary of War Belknap in 1875, implicating the president's own brother, Orville Grant, Custer's military career seemed over for the second time. But again a benefactor came to his defense: General Alfred Terry, commander of one of three units being assembled by General Sheridan to launch a determined campaign against the Indians that stretched across the entire West, interceded in Custer's behalf. By June 1876 Custer was once again leading the Seventh Cavalry against the Sioux.

Custer had, in fact, been instrumental in bringing the war against the Sioux to a boiling point, because it had been his much-publicized report in 1874 of the discovery of gold in the Black Hills that created a virtual stampede of eastern prospectors to the Dakotas, which, in turn, caused the government to tear up its previous guarantees to the Indians that their land would be protected. General Terry was given the assignment of waging war against the Sioux and driving them out of the Black Hills. He divided his regiment into three forces, took command of one column, and gave Custer and General John Gibbon command of the other two. Custer's orders were to drive the Sioux into the trap set by Terry and Gibbon at the plain where the Big Horn and the Little Big Horn rivers meet and then wait to cut off their escape route to the Big Horn Mountains.

Custer, knew, however, that following these orders would not result in a glorious personal victory, would not get him out of trouble with his superiors, and would not further his political career. So when Custer moved out on June 22, he was intent not in driving the Sioux but in destroying them. Toward that end, he divided his own troops into the same kind of three-pronged attack

Years after the Battle of the Little Big Horn, Indian warriors who fought in the battle were photographed, usually with a feathered wand symbolizing the victory.

as Terry had done, with himself leading one column, and the others led by Major Marcus A. Reno and Frederick W. Benteen. This time, it was important for Custer to find the Sioux encampment before Terry, so he sent out scouts, including his favorite, Lonesome Charley Reynolds. They found the Sioux encamped at the Little Big Horn River and reported back to Custer that it was the largest encampment of Indians they had ever seen.

In fact, it was one of the largest number of Indians to gather in one place up to that time: between ten thousand and fifteen thousand Sioux and Cheyenne, including nearly four thousand fighting men. Custer was urged to stay with Terry's plan and not to attack, especially not in the heat of the day after his men had marched for several days in the hot sun. But Custer knew time was short, and if he was to make his move, it would have to be right then, on the afternoon of June 25. Major Reno had been given the order to attack with his 225 men from the flank and drive the Indians toward

Custer's column of about the same size. Reno and his men advanced but were repulsed by the large number of Indian warriors. The contingent of Indians was so large that Custer suddenly found himself surrounded. Custer and his regiment were killed quickly that afternoon, while Reno and Benteen dug in for a siege that would last through the night and all of the next day.

By the time Terry and Gibbon arrived, Custer and his men had become part of history, and only a few survivors were still entrenched when the sun set on June 26. In the months that followed, the Battle of the Little Big Horn was elevated to the status of legend, and Custer was lionized as a martyr by those who promoted increased war with the Indians. The shock of the decimation of the Seventh Cavalry was so great that rumors inevitably arose that the fault lay with Major Reno, who, it was alleged, had panicked and retreated. There was, indeed, clear indication that Reno panicked when his chief scout, Bloody Knife, was killed early in the charge across the Little Big Horn and that this had caused him to retreat back across the river. It seemed that Reno and Custer were each waiting for the other to come and support his position, only neither was able to move against the waves of the attacking Sioux and Cheyenne.

Of the film depictions of Custer, the portrayal by Ronald Reagan (second from left), here playing Custer as a West Point cadet, may unwittingly have been the most accurate.

A military court of inquiry was convened at Reno's request to clear up what happened, but the evidence was scanty and contradictory. Reno was cleared, but his reputation never recovered.

As for Custer, questions arose afterward about his fitness to command and about the role his arrogance and ambition had played in the massacre; some whispered that Custer, realizing he had made a gross miscalculation, took the coward's way out and shot himself on the battlefield. This story received support from the fact that his body was found with a bullet in the head, and unscalped (it was the custom of Indian warriors not to scalp a fallen soldier if he was already dead). But Custer also had a champion in the person of his wife, Libbie, who spent the next fifty-seven years writing books, lecturing, and defending her late husband. Much of what she wrote was inaccurate or misleading, especially her denial that her husband had had political aspirations.

It took quite some time to undo the damage, but in the latter half of the twentieth century, a clearer picture of the man emerged; it now appears that General Custer was more complex than it is healthy for most soldiers to be. Historical treatments of the event and the man slowly probed the inner workings of both and reevaluated the entire conduct of federal policy toward the Native Americans. Frederic Van De Water's 1934 work, *Glory Hunter*, set the tone for later interpretations, brought forward step by step by such authors as Robert Utley in his 1969 work, *Custer's Battlefield*, and Dee Brown in the 1971 classic *Bury My Heart at Wounded Knee*, and reaching a climax in the 1984 best-seller by Evan S. Connell, *Son of the Morning Star*.

One can witness the change in American attitudes in the evolution of Custer por-

trayals in more than fifty years of film. The two early films—*Santa Fe Trail*, directed by Michael Curtiz in 1940, in which Custer is portrayed by a feckless Ronald Reagan, and the next year's *They Died with Their Boots On*, directed by Raoul Walsh, with a dashing and ebullient Errol Flynn as Custer—represent the pictures that Libbie Custer would have liked us to accept. As late as 1968, there is still something sympathetic to be found in Robert Shaw's performance in *Custer of the West*. But a breakthrough came in 1970, with Arthur Penn's *Little Big Man*. Richard Mulligan's portrayal of Custer was odd and not very historical, but it was tinged with all the dark corners one had always suspected lay beneath those golden locks. When a television movie based on the Connell book was made in 1991, the transformation was complete; Gary Cole's swaggering, neurotic Custer became an image of the man that this generation could call its own.

WILLIAM C. QUANTRILL.

During the Civil War, a band of guerrillas known as Quantrill's Raiders roamed the Midwest. The band was led by an Ohioan named William Quantrill, a figure who has spawned a great deal of speculation—mainly regarding whether or not he was sane. As one might imagine, Quantrill's name struck fear in many towns in the Missouri-Kansas region. Finally the Confederate Army (for whose cause Quantrill claimed to be fighting) issued orders that the man was to be shot on sight. The legacy that he left was so pervasive that later historians saw him as

William C. Quantrill, Missouri guerrilla chief during the Civil War.

the founder of the large-scale outlaw tradition that reached its climax during the gangster era of the 1920s. In other words, some saw a lineage of sorts from Quantrill to Al Capone.

William Clarke Quantrill was born on July 31, 1837, in Canal Dover, Ohio. He worked for a time as a schoolteacher, and it seems he taught "tinkering"—repairing metal household utensils—which he learned from his enterprising father, Thomas Henry Quantrill. The elder Quantrill even wrote a book, *A Tinker's Guide*, which William sold and which became a strong seller in the midwestern states.

William was reputed to be a strange child—stories abounded of his cruelty to animals. When he was still a teenager, he was thought to have killed a man, an act that forced him to flee westward in 1855. After prospecting unsuccessfully in the Pike's Peak area, he moved to Lawrence, Kansas, in 1859, where he lived under the alias Charley Hart.

During the sixteen months Quantrill spent in Lawrence, he supported himself through two activities: he captured runaway slaves and returned them for posted rewards, and he engaged in horse stealing, burglary, and arson. In January 1861, the U.S. marshal finally went after him, and he was forced to flee once again. When war broke out on April 12, 1861, Quantrill happened to be hiding out in Cherokee country. He joined the Confederate forces then under the command of General Ben McCulloch, but he wasn't cut out for army discipline and he was soon operating on his own. Quantrill was a magnet that attracted every misfit, criminal, psychotic, and murderer in the Missouri-Kansas region. Many of these men were uncontrollable by anyone, including Quantrill, and would not have even understood the impassioned justification Quantrill gave for his outfit's actions. Raids were also periodically being made at the time by the antislavery and pro-Unionist Kansas "jayhawkers." Although these raids were directed most often at military targets in the vaguely allied Kansas-Missouri border areas, they could be violent and sometimes resulted in the killing of disinterested bystanders. But nothing the jayhawkers did could have prepared anyone for Quantrill's Raiders.

Armed with Colt .45 guns and adept as horsemen, the raiders were a force to be reckoned with on the military scene, because they conducted devastating raids against cavalry units and armories. But their most notorious activities were the raids against and massacres of entire towns unsympathetic to the Confederacy. The most heinous of these raids was against the town of Lawrence, Kansas, Quantrill's old haunt and probably a town toward which he bore a great deal of resentment. On August 20, 1863, Quantrill and a force of between five hundred and nine hundred men surrounded the town and then rode in for a day of killing and pillaging. Some two

hundred citizens of the town of two thousand were killed; businesses and the bank were stripped of anything of value; and the buildings were set ablaze, lighting up the night sky. No doubt the entire town would have been massacred had a lookout not informed Quantrill that a large Union regiment was headed their way.

In 1865 Quantrill made his way east with the intention of winding up in Washington and assassinating President Lincoln. But Lincoln was assassinated by John Wilkes Booth on April 14 while Quantrill was terrorizing towns in Kentucky. Quantrill was finally captured on May 10, 1865, by troops under the command of Captain Edward Terrill, and he died of wounds he sustained during his capture. Quantrill had four thousand dollars on him when he was captured: he gave half to the priest who administered his last rites, and the other half to a Kate King, a woman he had kidnapped a few years earlier and who willingly became his mistress. King used her share of the money to open a brothel in St. Louis, Missouri.

For all his murderous insanity, Quantrill was remembered fondly by the "alumni" of his Raiders and by their sympathizers, and annual meetings of these "fans"—loosely associated with Ku Klux Klan activities—were held into the 1920s. For many years, the Kansas State Historical Society displayed bones that were said to have been Quantrill's, and which were taken from his grave when it was displaced during the 1870s.

Quantrill was very rarely portrayed in film, his particular brand of psychosis being too much even for the excesses of Hollywood. He was portrayed darkly (and oddly) by Walter Pidgeon in the 1940 film *Dark Command*, in which he was the villainous foil for John Wayne. In 1951 he was portrayed by John Ireland in a minor film, *Red Mountain*. The main fascination with Quantrill seems to have been his ability to train men who would later become famous outlaws of the West, such as Jesse James and Cole Younger. There definitely was a methodology to his raids, and he brought military tactics to the murderous business of robbery and terror. Some of his Raiders went off to form bands of heir own— "Bloody" Bill Anderson and George Todd are two examples. And a similar pro-Union outfit was created and led by James H. Lane. But in this postwar period, Quantrill was without equal as an invoker of terror throughout the Midwest.

SANTA ANNA

Antonio Lopez de Santa Anna, Mexico's most decorated general, victor at the Alamo, and loser at the Battle of San Jacinto.

Not all the generals commanding troops in the West were American; the United States fought a sporadic war with Mexico between 1836 and 1848. Fighting sometimes flared in Texas (as part of the war for Texas independence), sometimes in California (during the Bear Flag Rebellion), and sometimes in Mexico itself. The Mexican government was divided into factions with different loyalties toward Spain (much as the American colonists were divided in their attitudes toward England a half century earlier), and this divisiveness played into American hands

While the Mexicans were fighting on their own territory from well-developed cities, the U.S. forces were camped on foreign soil. This depiction of Zachary Taylor's camp at Walnut Springs, near Monterrey, Mexico, was created in 1847.

at key points during the war. The one common factor throughout the dozen years of war was the military leadership of the Mexican forces by one man: Antonio Lopez de Santa Anna.

Santa Anna is famous in history and lore as the Mexican general who led the charge on the Alamo (described in greater detail in the section on Davy Crockett). The villainous image that episode has left of him is complemented by the equally unflattering image of Santa Anna dressed as a pauper trying to escape capture by Sam Houston's troops at the Battle of San Jacinto. But he was an important part of Mexican politics

for three decades and was, until the defeats of his later years, a glorified hero of the Mexican people. Santa Anna's political strategy, which he followed his entire lifetime virtually to the day he died, was to offer his services and loyalties to both sides of every issue. He became famous in Mexico for fighting alongside Augustin de Iturbide in the Mexican War of Independence in 1821; two years later, he helped depose Iturbide and later supported Vicente Guerrero's ascendance to power, only to oppose him later. Given the quixotic nature of Santa Anna's loyalties, it is frankly amazing that he did not offer to fight *for* Texas independence at the same time that he actually was fighting against it.

Santa Anna became a hero of Mexico in 1829, when he defeated the Spanish in their attempt to reconquer Mexico. The "Hero of Tampico," as he was known, rose to the presidency in 1833. He ruled the country with near-dictatorial powers as an anti-Church federalist and assumed direct control of the Mexican Army. His march into Texas in 1836 was aimed at punishing American settlers for declaring their independence; in fact, the declaration was taken seriously neither in Mexico nor in Washington. The U.S. government was, at the time, much more concerned with the acquisition of Florida, and there was a feeling that Texas was going to wind up as part of the United States in due time. In fact, when events led to Texas's independence sooner than anyone expected, the area had to become an independent country while the issue of annexation was hashed out back in Washington.

Santa Anna, fancying himself the "Napoleon of the West," achieved victory at the Alamo and again later at Goliad. But he was defeated by a small force of Texans led by Sam Houston at the Battle of San Jacinto on April 21, 1836, in one of the most stunningly lopsided military victories since the Battle of Agincourt. Santa Anna was captured and spared by Houston and was then sent to Washington, where he met with President Andrew Jackson. It was an apparently embarrassing meeting for all parties concerned, because the United States was not yet ready to annex Texas and Mexico was not prepared to concede defeat. Santa Anna was sent back to Mexico on the condition that he retire, a condition he abided by for all of two years. When the French seized the port of Veracruz, Santa Anna was called out of retirement to lead the Mexican forces against them. The encounter was not much of a battle; the French retreated as soon as they realized the Mexicans were going to mount an all-out offensive, but Santa Anna lost a leg in the brief skirmish.

Santa Anna became president of Mexico briefly in 1839 and then again in 1841 as the leader of a revolt. He remained president

The Battle of Chapultepec, September 18, 1847, as depicted in a Currier & Ives lithograph.

until 1845, when he was driven into exile after losing the war with the United States.

The Mexican War began in April 1846, and it made heroes of a number of U.S. generals, one of whom, Zachary Taylor, later became president. Other generals became battle-ready for the roles they would play back east in the coming Civil War. The battles themselves, especially those that took place above the Rio Grande and along the Pacific coast, held a certain absurdity, because the majority of the inhabitants of these territories were American settlers. Throughout the Southwest, the ratio of Americans to Mexicans was at least ten to one, often greater. The politicians in Washington believed a war was not necessary because the demographics were going to make these areas U.S. possessions sooner or later, and the Mexicans were more interested in saving face than in substantiating their claim to the land.

When war finally was declared, even President Polk was surprised, because he had personally sent Santa Anna on a peace mission. But he was double-crossed by the Mexican general, and when Winfield Scott marched his troops into Mexico, he once again found the Mexican Army commanded by Santa Anna. Three defeats of Santa Anna's forces—at the battles of Buena Vista, Cerro Gordo, and Chapultepec—ended Santa Anna's career in Mexican politics. He went into exile, first in Venezuela, and then Jamaica, returning to Mexico several times over the next decade, only to be driven out. In 1863 he sought American support in overthrowing Maximilian, the "emperor" placed on the throne of Mexico by the French, though, characteristically, he also offered his services to Maximilian. Both turned him down, and he was exiled once again. In 1867 Santa Anna settled in the United States, and only in 1874 was he allowed to return to Mexico; by then he was

old and blind. He died in Mexico City on June 21, 1876.

In most of the early literature and film portrayals, Santa Anna is an anonymous figure—a faceless leader of the horde of Mexican troops that overran the Alamo and slept through Sam Houston's attack at San Jacinto. But Santa Anna led an interesting life and played a significant role in the history of the American West beyond the events surrounding the Battle of the Alamo. Not until the character of Santa Anna was given some dimension in the 1958 book *Thirteen Days to Glory: The Siege of the Alamo*, by J. Lon Tinkle, did aficionados of the period realize that he was worth investigating. The Tinkle book was turned into a made-for-cable-television movie, *The Alamo: 13 Days to Glory*, the most interesting part of which was the rousing and flamboyant portrayal of Santa Anna by Raul Julia.

GEORGE CROOK

In carrying out the government's policy toward the Indians, three generals show that a wide range of action was available to field commanders. They could be compassionate and fair or ruthless and mendacious, with gradations in between. The career of General George Crook illustrates the first style; Nelson Miles represents the tenacious and ruthless pursuit of the Indians; and John Chivington dealt with the Indians with treachery and inhuman ferocity. All three found their supporters at the highest levels of government and among the general population.

In all his dealings with tribal leaders, George Crook made every effort to be truthful and to see that the Indians were treated fairly. As a result, he was respected and revered by the Indians, and they eventually gave him the name "Chief Grey Wolf" as an indication of their respect. The U.S. Army also appreciated Crook's management of Indian affairs, and General Sherman called him the "greatest Indian fighter and manager the army ever had." Crook often protected the Indians from the ignorance and racism of the agents of the Department of the Interior who generally regarded the Indians as animals to be confined to reserves (or "reservations"—a double-edged word that meant land set aside for the Indian but also connoted something akin to animal refuges).

After graduating West Point near the bottom of his class, Crook served for eight years as commander of the Fourth Infantry stationed in California. During this period, he learned a great deal about the mentality of the West, the plight of the Indians, and the general drunkenness and untrustworthiness of the army. The Civil War brought Crook back east, where he used his experience to train guerrilla units in securing the backlands of West Virginia. He distinguished himself at the second Battle of Bull Run and again in the Shenandoah Campaign of 1864. By the end of the war, he was a major general.

In the reorganization of the army following the war, Crook was appointed lieutenant colonel, in command of the Twenty-third Infantry, and ordered to suppress the Indian uprising in the Boise district of Idaho. Crook waged a two-year guerrilla campaign that completely pacified the region without much bloodshed on either side. When the more militant Indians of the Southwest proved to be too much for Colonel George Stoneman, President Grant put Crook in command of the Department of Arizona in 1871.

General George Crook.

Crook's style of command was always considered unorthodox—"unsoldierly" was another word often applied—but his insistence on being on the front lines and not in the safety of a rear command position made him much admired in President Grant's administration. He set aside the usual trappings of generalship while on maneuvers, living with his men and wearing a pith helmet and a plain canvas suit instead of the military regalia. Crook preferred riding a mule and demonstrated the value of mule pack transport in several campaigns. He was famous for never swearing, smoking, or drinking either coffee or liquor, and he was approachable by officer and enlisted man alike, which made him both a respected and beloved commander. Crook looked after the welfare of his men, sometimes in opposition to orders, and this made his soldiers all the more loyal and dedicated.

Above: General Crook was not a conventional soldier, as this photograph shows: he looked more like a prospector-explorer with his two Apache scouts, Dulchy (left) and Alchise. Right: In newspaper depictions, such as this one showing Chief Nana entering Crook's camp to sue for peace, he was still shown in army uniform.

In two years of very active pressure against the Apaches, Crook had brought about a tense peace in which the Apaches were confined, though not on the reservations prescribed by the U.S. government. In 1875 Crook was put in command of the Department of the Platte, where he cleared the Black Hills of trespassing miners. He participated in the 1876 campaign against the Sioux, and it was then that he suffered the defeat at the Battle of the Rosebud. This battle was between Crook's force of twelve hundred and an equal number of Cheyenne and Sioux warriors led by Crazy Horse. Crook's column was one of the three that General Alfred Terry had hoped would wage a three-pronged assault on the Sioux.

On the one hand, Crook's defeat was surprising because he believed that his deployment was unknown to the Indians, whereas they had been following his progress for several days before the battle. On the other hand, when the two forces met, Crook's soldiers were sufficiently well trained in guerrilla fighting that they would not be subject to the same rout as Custer would experience later. The battle took place on June 17, 1876, and although it ended with both forces retreating (and Crook claiming it as a victory), the immobilization of his column deprived Terry of one prong of his attack, which set the scene for the massacre of the Seventh Cavalry led by Custer at the Little Big Horn.

Crook returned to Arizona, where the peace he had established was being stretched beyond the breaking point. Crook had treated the Indians as human beings, keeping his word and protecting them from exploitation and even from the genocidal plots continually being hatched by the Department of the Interior. Crook's policy was seen as effective in the short run, but there was a feeling that the peace Crook had forged also gave the Indians a respite in which to mount a campaign against the American settlements of the Southwest.

In March 1886 Crook pressured the Chiracahua to formally surrender, and he arrested their chief, the famous Geronimo. Geronimo and his band were allowed to return unescorted to the reservation, but instead they fled to the mountains and continued their raids. Crook was sorely criticized for mishandling Geronimo, though the same policies had been praised earlier. It signaled a shift in government policy and a determination that the time had come to abandon Crook's humane approach in favor of a more direct line of attack. Crook was replaced by Nelson Miles. In the last years of his life, Crook became a tireless worker on behalf of Indian rights and humane treatment of the Indians, writing, lecturing, and conducting a campaign against Nelson Miles's treatment of the Indians. He campaigned for "allotment," a plan allowing Indians to own private parcels of land on the reservation, which he believed would help protect their rights and incorporate them into American society. He died in Chicago in 1890, and was mourned both by infantry soldiers and officers and by leaders of the Sioux and Apache nations. It is unbelievable that so colorful and heroic a figure has failed to attract the attention of historical novelists or filmmakers. Several books investigate his exploits, character, and the Battle of the Rosebud (such as *On the Border with Crook*, by John Bourke, published in 1891), and an autobiography was edited by Martin Schmitt and published by the University of Oklahoma in 1946. But the only film to have paid tribute to the general is the little-known *Walk the Proud Land* (1956), in which Audie Murphy played a character loosely based on Crook.

NELSON MILES

Georg Crook's chief rival was a military man who had not been a West Point graduate but instead had risen through the ranks. Nelson Appleton Miles, a Massachusetts-born shopkeeper, had received the Congressional Medal of Honor for his actions at Chancellorsville in 1863. After the war, he went west as a colonel in command of the Fifth Infantry, and he defeated Comanche, Kiowa, and Cheyenne tribes in the Red River War of 1874–75. In 1876 he joined George Crook in the war against the Sioux, and in 1877 he raced after the Nez Percé Indians as they fled toward Canada, catching up with them just thirty miles from the border and forcing Chief Joseph to surrender.

In the Sioux campaign, the difference between the approaches of Miles and Crook became apparent—to the Indians no less than to the bureaucrats in Washington—and friction arose between these two commanders. Many of the defeats suffered by the Sioux at the hands of Miles resulted in their surrender to Crook, whom they trusted and who they knew would treat them fairly. Miles was an intensely ambitious man who wanted nothing else but to one

General Nelson Miles.

day become general of the army, and he chafed at the credit he felt Crook had received at his expense.

When Geronimo bolted for the mountains after promising Crook he would make straight for the reservation, the Department of the Interior, looking to step up the aggressiveness of the war against the Indians, prevailed upon the army to replace Crook with Miles as commander of the Department of Arizona. Miles immediately set out to capture Geronimo with the same relentless pursuit with which he had vanquished the Nez Percé. But unlike Crook, who relied heavily

An 1892 etching showing General Nelson Miles finding a message left for him by Chief Sitting Bull. Such messages were generally regarded as threatening regardless of the content.

on Indian scouts and on his knowledge of what he called "the Indian within," Miles used primarily his own army scouts and a system of observation posts that communicated with one another with a heliographic signaling device. He regarded the Indians as he would any other enemy, without regard for the fact that they had been the original inhabitants of the land.

Miles and his troops pursued Geronimo and his band of about forty Apaches through the Sierra Madre and across the entire Southwest, logging more than three thousand miles (4,800km) over a five-month period, without coming any closer to capturing (or sighting) Geronimo. Miles finally sent Lieutenant Charles Gatewood

and several Apache scouts to contact Geronimo and offer him terms of surrender. Miles had been given orders to demand an unconditional surrender, but realizing this was not possible, he offered Geronimo terms that would allow him and his band to travel (this time escorted) to a reservation in Florida. Inexplicably (though possibly to see to it that Lieutenant Gatewood did not receive credit for the surrender), Miles also sent the Apache scouts to the reservation, even though they had been loyal to him and were enlistees of the U.S. Army.

Miles was made commander of the Military Division of the Missouri in 1890, a post previously held by generals Sherman and Sheridan—one that he believed would soon catapult him to the post of commanding general of the army. He took personal command of the army's suppression of the Ghost Dance uprising in 1890 and was in close contact with the field commander of the Seventh Cavalry, Colonel James W. Forsyth, during its maneuvers. The massacre of one hundred and fifty Sioux men, women, and children on the Pine Ridge Reservation on Wounded Knee Creek, South Dakota, seemed to have been a spontaneous action by cavalry members during a period when Forsyth had momentarily lost control of his troops, but the policy and the intent of the unit had already been expressed by Miles and was included in the aggressively worded marching orders of the commanders.

Fearing the incident would jeopardize his chances of promotion, Miles distanced himself from the massacre and chastised Forsyth for the actions of his cavalrymen. A court of inquiry was convened, and Forsyth was relieved of command. The secretary of war intervened and restored Forsyth, and Wounded Knee was forgotten.

In 1895, after acquitting himself in putting down the riots arising out of the

Pullman strikes of 1894, Miles was made commander of the army. The administrations of William McKinley and Theodore Roosevelt did not think highly of Miles; to them he was a pompous, vain anachronism of a bygone century. During the Spanish-American War, he was not permitted to lead the American Expeditionary Force to Cuba; instead he was sent to Puerto Rico, where he saw little action. Seeing that he was no longer a factor in politics or the military, he retired in 1903. Nelson Miles lived in Washington, D.C., to the ripe old age of eighty-six; he died on May 25, 1925.

Miles wrote two books of memoirs; a biography of him by Virginia W. Johnson, *The Unregimented General*, was published in 1962. Miles spent much of his life seeking military honors—he never stopped arguing that it was he and not Crook who had defeated the Sioux and Geronimo, and he carried on a bitter feud with General Oliver Otis Howard over credit for the surrender of the Nez Percé. For all his vanity and pomposity, he chided West Point officers for their military bearing and for the advantage he claimed they had in receiving promotions. His attitude toward the Indians never changed, in spite of his outrage at the Wounded Knee Massacre.

JOHN M. CHIVINGTON

Beyond even Nelson Miles in his hatred and ruthless treatment of the Indians was Colonel John M. Chivington, known as the "Fighting Parson," because he was a Methodist minister. Chivington was born in 1821 in Ohio. He became a blacksmith, a profession befitting his six-foot, seven-inch frame. He was of Irish extraction and was known to be loud and hot-tempered whether he was preaching the gospel or ranting against the ungodly heathens, the Indians. After roaming the Midwest preaching, Chivington found an environment in which he could thrive: the mining areas of Colorado. He was so well received there that he soon got it into his head that he might one day become governor of Colorado.

When the Civil War began, the federal government could spare few troops to maintain order in the West and in fact looked westward for recruits to fight in the East. Coloradans, realizing that their best chance of staying alive was to stay in Colorado, did everything they could to instigate the Indians into uprisings and raiding. Chivington accepted a commission for the First Regiment (turning down an offer to serve as the regiment's chaplain), believing he would spend the war safely in

Prior to the Sand Creek Massacre, a group of Cheyenne men, women, and children entered Fort Lyon, Colorado, and sued for peace.

Colorado. In the summer of 1861, the First Regiment received a call for help from Union forces pinned down by the Confederates in New Mexico. Chivington led a force of men through the mountains and attacked the Confederate forces at La Glorieta Pass from the rear. The action was deemed a turning point in the war in the West, and Chivington suddenly found himself a war hero.

After the war, Chivington commanded the Third Colorado Cavalry, a volunteer group drawn mostly from the mining towns and organized specifically to quell the Indian uprisings in the territory. In late November 1864, a force of some one thousand soldiers of the Third Cavalry set out from Fort Lyon with the intent of attacking the Cheyenne village on the banks of Sand Creek, located some thirty miles north. The chief of the village, Black Kettle, had been guaranteed safety by the commander of Fort Lyon, Major E.W. Wyncoop, and was told that as long as he flew the Union flag outside his tent, no harm would come to him and his village.

As the soldiers neared the camp, Indian braves alerted Black Kettle to their presence; Black Kettle assured them that they had nothing to fear as long as the flag was visible to the soldiers (and it assuredly was). As the soldiers started their charge, a white man living among the Cheyenne, John Simpson Smith, ran out toward the soldiers, hoping to stop them. He was cut down by gunfire, the first casualty of the charge. The devastation that followed was enough to make people sick: not only were all the people in the camp—every man, woman, and child—slaughtered, but many rapes were committed, and many of the dead were sexually mutilated. When the raid ended, more than five hundred Cheyenne lay dead as the howling soldiers rode off, frozen scalps dangling from their saddles.

Chivington was clearly proud of his men and of the massacre. He wrote that it was "unnecessary to report that I captured no prisoners." But the government could not ignore the atrocity, and Chivington was court-martialed. His actions were condemned, but he was acquitted (on the technicality that he had resigned from the army before trial) and simply relieved of his command. He remained a prominent figure in Denver political life, serving as the under-sheriff until his death in 1894.

JOHN C. FRÉMONT

Before any of the fighting, some soldiers explored the West and opened it to settlers (who then commenced to do the fighting). Although John Charles Frémont is not as famous as Lewis and Clark or Zebulon Pike, this soldier most assuredly deserves to be placed alongside them as pioneer explorer and pathfinder into the wilderness of the western United States. He was, in fact, given the epithet "The Pathfinder," and he remained committed to exploration and opening up the West to his dying day. His career is one of the more exciting of the period—and his wife, Jessie Benton Frémont, led an interesting life of her own.

The child of Frenchman Charles Frémon and Richmond socialite Ann Whiting, John Charles Frémont was born out of wedlock in 1813. The scandal of Ann leaving her older husband to run off with her French lover had rocked all of Virginia, but the couple were to have three children, John Charles being the eldest. John was a brilliant, if rambunctious, student, and he

General John C. Frémont, celebrated explorer of the Oregon Trail, in 1893.

received his bachelor's degree in mathematics in 1836, after a delay of five years to clear up some disciplinary problems. In 1833 Frémont (the *t* was added to his name to Americanize it) taught mathematics to sailors on the U.S.S. *Natchez,* and in 1836–37 he assisted on surveys for the Charleston and Cincinnati Railroad. In 1838 he was made a second lieutenant in the U.S. Corps of Topographical Engineers and was assigned to assist Joseph N. Nicollet in his survey of the upper Mississippi and Missouri rivers.

Frémont accompanied Nicollet on two surveys of the vast area between the two rivers and south of the Canadian border. He became the elderly scientist's right hand and was invaluable in helping him draw up the famous Nicollet Map when they returned to Washington. It was on this trip

Jessie Benton Frémont, author of the writings that brought fame to her husband and to his scout, Kit Carson.

the expedition were several: one was to open up the western territories to further settlement; another was to encourage easterners with the opportunities that lay out West; and yet another was to begin the process of laying claim to the Oregon territory then jointly claimed by England and the United States.

Frémont set out on this expedition (as he did on his later expeditions) from St. Louis–Independence, Missouri. The expedition took Frémont up the Platte River. The group explored the two forks of the Platte—the North Platte and the South Platte—and then followed the Sweetwater River to its source in the Wind River Mountains. On this trip, he took along twenty-one voyageurs (fur traders who were usually French Canadians and familiar with the ways of the woodlands), the cartographer Charles Preuss, a hunter named Lucian Maxwell, and as guide a young man named Christopher "Kit" Carson, whom Frémont had just met, but who had been a friend and student of early mountain man Joe Walker. Frémont was also equipped with the latest surveying equipment and a daguerreotype camera.

When the expedition reached South Pass, the gateway to Oregon, Frémont was disappointed to find it a gently sloping ridge of only about seventy-five hundred feet (2,286m) in elevation. He was determined to climb something more dramatic, and though there were clearly many other peaks within sight that were taller, he selected a mountain 13,785 feet (4,201.7m) high (since named Mount Frémont in his honor), climbed it, and declared it the tallest in the Rockies. When he returned to Washington, he sat down to record his adventures and draw a definitive map from his notes. And he made what may have been his most startling discovery: he could not write nearly as well as his wife, Jessie.

to Washington that Frémont met Jessie Anne Benton, the beautiful and ebullient seventeen-year-old daughter of Thomas Hart Benton, a powerful senator from Missouri. Although John and Jessie had eloped, the senator was supportive of Frémont and defended his son-in-law when he later came under fire in Washington.

In 1842 Frémont was sent on his first expedition into the uncharted West. It was not an accident that Frémont was chosen for the mission. In addition to Frémont's experience assisting Nicollet, Senator Benton had urged Congress to appropriate thirty thousand dollars for the expedition and to appoint Frémont its head. The purposes of

Left: Joseph Nicollet, an important explorer of the West, at Lake Itasca in 1840. Below: The dime novels of Beadle & Adams, wildly successful in the late 1800s, were an important source of information (and misinformation) about the West in the eastern portion of the country.

The 207-page report, largely ghostwritten by Jessie Frémont, was so exciting and captivating—factually compelling with poetic passages of discovery and insight—that Congress ordered ten thousand copies to be printed and distributed.

Frémont had little trouble getting financial backing from Congress for a second expedition, though it viewed his request for a Howitzer cannon with alarm. The idea of Frémont wandering around the West with a cannon that could start a war with Mexico was unsettling. But he insisted (he claimed he needed it to frighten off the Indians, but those close to him felt he simply enjoyed the image of leading an entourage equipped with a formidable implement of war) and set out on his second expedition in 1844. His instructions were to extend his original track beyond South Pass to Oregon and connect with the northwestern path charted by Commander Charles Wilkes in 1841 from Fort Vancouver to San Francisco. This would have given the army a clear and useful idea of the terrain from the Mississippi clear to the Pacific. Frémont did this, but then, in an expedition that lasted fourteen months, he did much more. Having charted a trail through Fort Bridger,

An 1864 presidential campaign poster, in the form of a color lithograph by Currier & Ives, for "Radical Democracy" candidates John C. Frémont and General John Cochrane.

Basin to Utah Lake (a freshwater lake Frémont mistakenly thought was the Great Salt Lake); and went through the Uinta Mountains to Pike's Peak and then back to Independence. Frémont had made a complete circuit of the West and had returned with a wealth of information, most (but not all) of it factual. He issued another report—with the generous assistance of Preuss and Jessie Frémont—which was even more sensational than the first. It opened up the Oregon Trail and changed forever the image people had of the West, encouraging settlement in virtually every area. Frémont's second report was largely responsible for the Mormons selecting Utah to settle in, which prompted Brigham Young's belief that Frémont must have been either an idiot or a liar.

Frémont embarked on a third expedition, with both Carson and Walker as his guides, and this time with very clear instructions from the Bureau of Topographical Engineers. They wanted him to map the areas "within a reasonable distance to Bent's Fort," which would have been helpful in planning expansion of the Santa Fe Trail and could have laid the foundation for a railroad line to the Pacific coast. Frémont followed instructions, and then, claiming he was acting under orders, he again continued westward to the Sierra Nevada and then south to the Mojave. This time he did encounter opposition from Mexican officials, who were leery of a large military contingent so close to Mexico. Frémont turned north and arrived in Monterey in time to join the Bear Flag Rebellion against Mexico. He assembled a makeshift group known as the California Battalion, and after overpowering the weak Mexican presence, he was appointed governor of California. This glory lasted until official representation of the U.S. government arrived in the person of General Stephen

Fort Hall, Fort Boise, Whitman Mission, and Fort Vancouver, instead of returning home along the same path, he turned south along the eastern slopes of the Cascade Mountains. He crossed the barren region of the Great Basin (which he was the first to accurately describe and identify accurately); crossed the Sierra Nevada (with the help of Joe Walker, who met them en route and who led them through a pass still unidentified) to Sutter's Fort, where he was refitted—the Howitzer having been abandoned in a snowdrift while the expedition was crossing the mountains; continued south through the San Joaquin Valley; turned left and crossed the Mojave Desert; continued up the south ridge of the Great

Kearny. Frémont bristled at Kearny's order that he disband his unit and step down, and Kearny (with a legendary hot temper of his own) had Frémont arrested and sent back to Washington for court-martial. The trial was a blustery affair, with Senator Benton using every opportunity to make political hay of the matter, but Frémont was found guilty. President Polk, hoping to mend some fences, offered to pardon Frémont and return him to duty, but Frémont refused and resigned his commission in disgust.

Frémont made two other expeditions in the West, both for the purpose of finding railroad routes; both failed miserably (and one disastrously, with the loss of ten men in the mountain snows). He was also given a large tract of California land in 1847 that turned out to have rich veins of gold, but Frémont so mismanaged its development that he soon lost the land to pay off his creditors. Frémont served as senator from California in 1850, and in 1856 he was the first presidential nominee of the newly formed Republican party. He did surprisingly well, losing by only sixty electoral votes out of the 288 cast. During the Civil War, Frémont was made a general in charge of the Western Department. He lasted in this post for all of one hundred days, during which he issued foolish proclamations and ordered questionable maneuvers, and after which he was relieved by Lincoln. He was nominated again for the presidency in 1864, but he withdrew for the good of the party and to ensure Lincoln's reelection. He invested all he had in a scheme to create a railroad that would connect Memphis and San Diego, and when that went bankrupt, the Frémonts were left penniless. For a while, he was supported by his salary as governor of the territory of Arizona, in which capacity he served from 1878 to 1881. During the latter years of his life, Frémont was supported mainly by his wife's writing

and the pension he was able to arrange for having been a general of the army. Frémont lived his last years in a Manhattan boardinghouse, sick and poverty-stricken, depending almost entirely on the income from the books about his earlier exploits that Jessie could crank out.

Frémont died in New York City on July 13, 1890, at the age of seventy-seven. He was a short man, barely a hair over five feet tall—and throughout his life, he insisted that any photograph taken of him with someone else should show him standing and the other person sitting. To many, he was laughably vain and childishly unrealistic, and he often showed a complete disregard for others, even those who were closest to him. Joe Walker once described Frémont as "morally and physically the biggest coward I have ever known." He had shown a knack for garnering the support of the wealthy and the influential, but he was never able to parlay that into real power or a legitimate station. Official Washington considered him a lucky bungler who should have been thankful to the Lord for ever finding his way back home.

Yet Frémont's efforts were not in vain or unappreciated. After the wars—the Mexican and the Civil—the army engineers picked up where Frémont left off and by 1879 had completed a total survey of the entire West, filling in the gaps and correcting the errors in Frémont's work. Many of the wagon trains headed west in the second half of the nineteenth century were equipped with the reports and maps Frémont created, and many of these settlers read and reread the inspiring prose that had encouraged them to set out for the West to seek their fortunes in the first place. It is nothing short of amazing that popular culture has not found its way to this colorful and remarkable person, surrounded as he was by a veritable galaxy of interesting characters.

CHAPTER FOUR

HEAD-DRESSES

The Indians

The earliest confrontations between Europeans and Indians in the West involved disputes over fur-trapping territories. In the Maurer painting, The Last Shot, *a trapper barely manages to stop an attacking brave.*

The people referred to as Indians (or sometimes as Native Americans) are the descendants of people who, some twenty thousand years ago, traveled over the land-ice bridge that connected easternmost Asia and the northwestern corner of the North American continent. This was not the first time the receding glaciers afforded Asian hunters the opportunity to expand their hunting grounds into North America—a similar opening of the bridge into western Alaska occurred about sixteen thousand years earlier, and there was no doubt some migration in this period as well. There is also evidence that some migration to the Americas took place from the East: some Nordic seafarers may have been able to cross over the northern rim of the Atlantic, and there is even some evidence that some

African migration across the South Atlantic to South America may have taken place in early antiquity. One look at the overall diversity of physiological types and languages among the inhabitants of the Americas when Europeans first came makes it clear that there must have been many points of origins for their ancestry.

The story of how Columbus, believing he had landed on the Indian subcontinent, called the inhabitants who greeted him "Indians" has been told and retold; it is still unclear what the relationship is between that story and the truth. Overland trade and previous sea voyages around Africa provided a body of some information about what India was like and who lived there. Columbus knew better and was clearly trying to convince someone of something, but who of what is not clear. The American Indians never had a single term for their collective being—in the final analysis, this may have been the key that determined their future. The names by which they have become known were usually given them by enemy tribes or white settlers. They referred to themselves in terms that simply meant "people" or "friend"—though it is striking that many of these terms bear a resemblance to the term "Indian" and perhaps that is why (one speculates) this error of history was perpetuated.

The image that has been held by many generations of Americans of a vast continent only sparsely and loosely inhabited by virtually prehistoric peoples has, by now, been largely dispelled. Nearly every corner of the continent was inhabited by some five hundred different Indian nations, and the culture that developed was rich and insightful. With hindsight, we can look back and discern in the many diverse cultures of the American Indians attitudes and values that bespeak belief structures worthy of admiration: beliefs about the land and humankind's

relationship to it; beliefs about the inner chasms of the human personality and mind; and beliefs about personal morality, family loyalty, and group fidelity.

Unfortunately, looking back is about all we can do. In the course of three hundred years, from 1600 to 1900, the original Native American population (in both North and South America) of anywhere from 9 million

Above: This poster, issued after 1910, makes no apology for the seizure of lands once owned and occupied by the Indians of the Great Plains. Left: Native American cultures and religions were based on a profound respect for the balance of the forces of nature. Because of this, the Indians were careful not to deplete the buffalo herds by over-hunting.

to 112 million was decimated and destroyed, so that only a small remnant of that population—about a million in North America; perhaps twice that in South America—remains. A large portion of the Indian population was destroyed by diseases brought over by the Europeans against which the natives had no defense. Sometimes, Europeans even gave Indians gifts infested with these diseases as a means of destroying them.

The Indians had many notions that differed markedly from those of Europeans, and this was largely responsible for their succumbing to the whites. They held different ideas of what made a parcel of land the property of an individual or tribe, believing that ownership was determined by use, and not by formal boundaries or agreements. In the many images we have of Indian villages, there is rarely any sign of fencing or other individual territorial indications, although dwellings and utensils were marked with family and identifying symbols. In all the transactions conducted with Indians for the sale of land, it was clear (even then) that the Indians had no concept of private ownership to apply to such a sale; they believed that they were selling the whites the right to encroach on their hunting, herding, or growing territory.

Indians had an extremely high estimation of the worth of the individual. They would not, for example, sacrifice themselves for the sake of victory by fighting at night, because they believed that the soul of a warrior who died at night would not find rest in the afterlife. It was perfectly acceptable for a warrior to leave a war party to hunt for food for himself or his family, without fear of being accused of cowardice or dereliction. Of course, without a political concept of territory, there was no need to carry battle to its limits of mass extermination. A sound beating

This 1914 portrait of Many Tail Feathers, a Blackfoot Indian chief, by J. Scheuerle, shows the classic strong profile of the Sioux people.

made the point, and the defeated, unwilling to place themselves at risk for the sake of an abstraction, retreated to a more hospitable region.

The Indians of the West were already veterans of dealing with the Europeans of the East, or at least they were aware of what had happened to other Indians east of the Mississippi. Although the earliest encounters with whites were not threatening—because it is not easy for a wagonload of ordinary people to threaten tens of thousands of battle-ready warriors—the Indians were aware of white intentions, in some cases, even before the Americans were. While the concept of Manifest Destiny and the policy of westward expansion were being debated, Indian psychics and medicine men had visions of the land being overrun by whites, who were imagined as everything from rats to walking trees to walking mountains.

The Indians had little doubt about how the whites felt about them. They were aware of the fact that most whites believed in the frontier aphorism "The only good Indian is a dead Indian." That saying was attributed to General Philip Sheridan, who replaced General William T. Sherman as commander of the Division of the Missouri, the key territory west of the Mississippi. But he actually said, "The only good Indians I ever saw were dead." What is interesting is the circumstance in which he uttered those words. It was his reponse when he was introduced to a Comanche chief, who identified himself deferentially by saying, "Me Tosawi, good Indian." Southerners who knew Sheridan from his tenure as commander of Texas and Louisiana were not at all surprised by this tale of his tactlessness.

Sheridan made his feelings clear to anyone who would listen and promoted like-minded officers regardless of their competence (including Custer, who was,

This painting by Wimar depicts an Indian attack on a wagon full of settlers. In virtually all cases, Indians warned settlers that they were encroaching on Indian territory before attacking.

by then, washed up in the military). The years of Sheridan's command, 1867 to 1883, were critically tragic years for the Indians of the West. Sheridan gave explicit orders to his commanders to take no adult male Indians prisoner and to bring all captured women and children back to be enslaved. And this from a man who had had been a *Union* general during the Civil War. Sheridan realized how dependent the Indians, particularly those on the Great Plains, were on the buffalo herds, and he actively promoted the hunting of buffalo. He protected the hunting parties, even at the cost of protecting wagon trains and settlements.

Sheridan followed in the footsteps of his predecessor, the eminent Civil War general William Tecumseh Sherman. Sherman served as commander of the Division of the Missouri for only three years—1866 to 1869—but during that time he set the course of policy toward the Indians of the West that would be pursued relentlessly by Sheridan. Sherman was responsible for

having the entire issue of treatment of the Indians transferred from the Interior Department to the War Department. And, as commanding general of the army, he embarked on the kind of military development that would later allow Sheridan to wage war against the Sioux and the Apache. Some historians believed that Sherman was somehow disapproving of Sheridan's conduct of the Indian wars. But Sheridan's campaigns would not have been possible without the material support he received from Sherman.

In what follows, an attempt is made to discuss the major Indian nations of the West and some of their leaders. It is a daunting task to capture an entire civilization, especially in a period during which it is going down in flames. But this was an integral part of the West, and unfortunately, the resolution of the "Indian problem" is what ultimately made the West habitable for white settlers.

The portrayal of the American Indian in literature and on screen is probably the final insult white America has visited upon the land's native peoples. Many of the portrayals are so ridiculous and superficial that one could argue that it would be best to wipe the slate clean and start all over. The story of the Indian tribes, beset by a culture beyond their understanding yet trying to break through both white hatred and their own ignorance to deal with the white civilization taking over their land, contains elements that are simply beyond the ken of modern American filmmakers. Every now and then, a writer or filmmaker has captured something of the essence of the American Indian and has presented their inner world and the full dimensions of the tragedy. More often than not, however, filmmakers have presented Indians in plastic and stereotypical terms, proving in their failure the importance of writing—and filming—only that which one really knows.

THE APACHE:

MANGAS COLORADAS, COCHISE, AND GERONIMO

The term "Apache" refers to a group of six tribes located roughly in the southwestern portion of the North American continent. These Indians were easily distinguished from the other tribes in the area insofar as they were seminomadic in style and culture. That meant that they settled an area for a period, living mainly in temporary dwellings known as *wickiups*, which were designed to be easy to take down and set up elsewhere. It was not the case that they were genuinely nomadic and lived without set boundaries and claimed

territories or that they refrained from farming and developing settlements; they did all those things, but simply changed these boundaries and settlements periodically to suit their needs.

The tribe's name came (probably) from the Zuni word for "attacker" or "enemy"; the Apache called themselves the *Inde*, or "People." The other Indians in the area feared the Apache as they would any seminomadic tribe. Such groups often have little regard for the concepts of private property or territorial boundaries and are given to the settling of any dispute by violent means. The Apache were indeed cunning and fierce fighters, as the Spanish discovered. And while the transition in the southwestern North American continent from Spanish to American dominance saw the

An Apache chief who adopted the name James A. Garfield, in a colorized photograph taken in 1899.

The great Apache chief Cochise.

put on reservations as about being cleared out of their original hunting areas.

At first, the Apache reserved their hostilities for other Indian tribes and for the Mexicans. They were cordial and even friendly to the American settlers passing through the Southwest to California in the nineteenth century.

Early in the century, while under the leadership of Chief Mangas Coloradas, the Apache were the victims of an act of treachery. An American trapper named James Johnson invited the Apache to a feast in the Mexican town of Santa Rita del Cobre; in the midst of the revelry, he fired off hidden cannons that resulted in the death of four hundred Apache. Johnson wanted to collect their scalps and turn them in to the Mexicans for a reward. The Apache blamed the Mexicans and embarked on a campaign against them. A large measure of Mexico's willingness to allow Americans to settle in Texas and New Mexico was because the Mexicans were not about to make any inroads into Apache territory.

Mangas Coloradas—which means "Red Sleeves" in Spanish, after a cloak he wore— was an unusually tall and striking man from the Mimbrenos Apache tribe. He was said to be a man of imposing dignity. He was born sometime between 1790 and 1795. In 1846 he greeted General Stephen Watts Kearny at the Gila River when the general was on his way to California, and offered to join the general in the war against their common enemy, Mexico. Kearny respectfully declined the chief's offer.

In 1851 Mangas had his first taste of white treachery: he innocently wandered into an American mining camp and was seized by the miners and given a savage whipping. Mangas returned to his camp, and when he recovered, he led a raid against that camp and killed every living soul there. From that time on, the Apache

landed tribes—the Zuni, the Yuma, the Mohave, and the Pueblo Indians—in serious decline (and, in some cases, on the verge of extinction), the Apache were still thriving and still in control of their land. But when a people has a purely utilitarian view of "their land" and no concept of territorial sovereignty, they are going to have a great deal of difficulty dealing with a military power that does have such a concept. It seems safe to say that the Apache, unlike other Indians, never did come to understand this concept. From statements made by later leaders, the Apache gave evidence of being every bit as confused about being

did not tolerate miners of any nationality or ethnicity on their land, though they were still accepting of American settlers passing through and even of American farmers and ranchers, but not hunters.

As was customary, Mangas gave his eldest daughter in marriage to an Apache chief—Cochise, the handsome young chief of the Chiracahua tribe. Cochise was a bit less friendly than his father-in-law to the white American settlers who traveled through Apache Territory, undoubtedly because the younger man saw where the settlement would ultimately lead. But the main focus of Apache hostility was still on the Mexicans, who had already constructed a string of settlements along both sides of the Rio Grande.

Relations between the Apache and American settlers worsened and eventually led to war following an 1860 episode known as the Bascom Affair. In October of that year, a band of Apache attacked a ranch run by John Ward, an Irish immigrant. Ward was away at the time, and his Mexican wife, Jesusa, was left defending the ranch. The objective of the raid was not to kill anyone; the Apache frequently conducted such raids to confiscate live-stock they considered theirs (because they grazed on Apache land) or simply owner-less. During the raid, they kidnapped a twelve-year-old Mexican boy named Felix Tellez, whom the Wards had adopted. When Ward returned, he reported to the nearest cavalry post at Fort Buchanan that it had been Cochise who had taken Felix. In January 1861 Lieutenant George Bascom was sent to rescue the boy.

Bascom went to meet Cochise at his camp near Apache Pass and made the chief believe that he was coming in friendship. During the meeting, Bascom asked the chief about the Ward raid, and Cochise told him that it was not his party that had raided the Ward ranch and that he knew nothing about Felix. Bascom did not believe him and sur-rounded the tent, telling Cochise that he would be kept under arrest until the boy was returned. A fight broke out in which men on both sides were killed, and Cochise escaped. Bascom kept three of the Apache elders hostage, which prompted Cochise to take three white men hostage. Bascom may have been inexperienced with the ways of the Apache, because he gave Cochise an ultimatum that led the chief to believe that Bascom was going to kill the hostages if

The lands of the West were so rich in resources that the Americans of the eastern half of the continent could not bear to allow the land to remain unconquered. In time, the European hunters outnumbered the Plains Indians.

Felix was not produced. Cochise, unpracticed in the white man's art of negotiation, killed the hostages he had taken, which caused Bascom to kill his hostages—and thus the war began.

This bloody war, with the Apache on one side and the American army and the settlers of the Southwest on the other, lasted for twenty years. More than four thousand lives were lost and untold damage was done to both Indian and American property. In 1862 Mangas Coloradas joined forces with Cochise, and the entire Apache nation entered the war. In April 1861 many of the soldiers left to fight the Civil War, and the Apache mistakenly believed they had prevailed over the U.S. Army. (Why else would

all the soldiers leave?) But in 1862 the cavalry returned, under the command of General James S. Carlton, and retook the area, injuring Mangas in battle. Mangas escaped and hid while Cochise carried on the fight, but the old chief was finally captured in 1863 and imprisoned at Fort McLane, New Mexico. According to the official report, Mangas Coloradas was later killed while trying to escape, but eyewitness accounts indicated that he had been tortured by soldiers with red-hot bayonets and had been killed while trying to fend them off.

The war with Cochise continued until President Ulysses S. Grant sent General Oliver O. Howard to effect a peace with the Apache. Howard was helped by Tom Jeffords, a friend of the chief, in negotiating an end to the war in 1872. As a result, the Apache, by now consisting largely of the Chiracahua, were given a large reservation in Warm Springs, New Mexico. Jeffords was appointed their Indian agent. Cochise died in 1874, and the agreement "guaranteed" by the U.S. government was unilaterally discarded in 1876. The Chiracahua were moved to a smaller reservation in San Carlos, one of the hottest and most arid areas of New Mexico.

And what ever happened to young Felix? The story might well have ended there, and Felix would have been considered lost among the Apache. Only he was not lost. In the early 1880s, an Apache scout named Mickey Free, who was working for the U.S. Army as a member of the troop of Indian scouts commanded by Al Sieber, came forward and claimed that he was Felix Tellez. He told the army investigators (and you may be sure these claims were carefully investigated) that he had been kidnapped by a band of Apaches not associated with the Chiracahua and that Cochise had told Bascom the truth. The Apache had let the boy go a few years later, and he had worked

Mickey Free, in a posed photograph taken in 1881.

as a ranch hand and then as a scout. Photographs taken of Felix left no doubt that Mickey Free was telling the truth, and the United States was left to contemplate the awful truth that the decades of carnage in the American war with the Apache had been completely unnecessary.

Life in the San Carlos Reservation, meanwhile, was intolerable for the Apache, and some of them left to conduct a guerrilla war against the U.S. government. Led by two of Mangas Coloradas's lieutenants, Victorio and Nana, a band of one hundred and fifty Apache conducted raids against both Mexican and American settlements and escaped capture by hiding in the Candelaria Mountains of northern Mexico. When these two warriors were brought to heel— Victorio was killed along with eighty of his men by the Mexican Army in October 1880, and Nana surrendered to General George Crook in 1883 and returned to San Carlos— a medicine man rose to lead his people. He was known to his people as Goyathlay

("He Who Yawns"), but to the rest of the world as Geronimo (the Spanish equivalent of Jerome). His family had all been killed by Mexicans in 1858 during a raid on the town of Janos. Most of Geronimo's raids before the Bascom Affair were directed at Mexicans, and he, not being a Chiracahua but a Nednis Apache (although his second wife was a Chiracahua), did not have the kind of hatred of the Americans that Cochise's followers had. As a result, Geronimo was able to "play" the U.S.government more effectively, sometimes attacking U.S. installations as a renegade and sometimes allowing himself to be captured, only to be coddled and protected as a vaunted "prisoner of war."

Geronimo was not tall and muscular like the Apache chiefs who fought the Americans before him; he was of average height and build, with the piercing gaze that stood a

Above: Geronimo (1834–1909), the great Apache chief and warrior. His real name was Goyathlay—"He Who Yawns." Below: A later photograph of Geronimo, by then subdued and defeated.

The council between General Crook (second from right) and Geronimo (third from left). The fact that the General was willing to meet Geronimo on equal terms and without any intimidation was an indication of Crook's enlightened attitude toward his adversaries.

medicine man in good stead. In 1881 Geronimo and Nana led a band of Apache out of the San Carlos Reservation and began to terrorize the inhabitants of the Southwest on both sides of the border. In 1883 Geronimo took charge of the Apache band and equipped it with the latest rifles and field equipment, including binoculars taken from attacked army units (this would have been considered unconscionable by a "real" chief of the Apache). So effective had Geronimo become that allowing pursuit of Apache across the U.S.–Mexican border was one of the very few things upon which the two governments could agree.

In 1884 Geronimo surrendered to General Crook on his own terms, and after leaving the reservation again in 1885, he again surrendered to Crook in 1886 but bolted before being returned to the reservation. This caused the army to reassign the task of bringing Geronimo in to General Nelson Miles, who was not nearly as under-

standing a commander as Crook. Miles had little success finding Geronimo, whose marauding activities went on unabated. Miles finally resorted to using Apache scouts to communicate with Geronimo and convince him to accept an unconditional surrender. Geronimo, it later turned out, had not understood the "unconditional" part, but he insisted that his surrender be to the military authorities, which put him beyond the prosecution of the local justices. He was shipped to Florida, where he spent most of his time in a drunken stupor. He was transferred to Fort Sill, Oklahoma, and converted to Christianity. In the last years of his life, Geronimo became a sideshow attraction, selling autographed pictures of himself, touring as a performer in the Pawnee Bill Wild West Show, and serving as an "exhibition" at the 1901 Pan-American Exposition in Buffalo and at the St. Louis World's Fair of 1904. Before he died, Geronimo dictated an autobiography, which was edited by S. M. Barrett and published in 1906. Geronimo died in February 1909 at age seventy-five at Fort Sill; he was still on the government's payroll as a scout.

THE CHEYENNE AND THE ARAPAHO:

BLACK KETTLE, ROMAN NOSE, AND DULL KNIFE

There is a deep irony in the sad fate of the Cheyenne and Arapaho nations in the late 1880s. These two tribes, very different in their cultures yet connected politically because of their early alliance against both other Indian tribes and American settlers, began the 1700s as settled peoples, cultivating farms in well-established communities in Minnesota. By the end of the nineteenth century, after adapting to a nomadic lifestyle on the Plains with amazing speed, these peoples had been forced by the U.S. government back into a settled and sedentary lifestyle—on the reservation.

The two nations had different languages and many different customs—the Arapaho, for example, buried their dead in the ground; the Cheyenne placed them on above-ground biers. The Cheyenne were tall and muscular; the Arapaho tended to be shorter and stockier. Cheyenne men were noted for being handsome and athletic; Cheyenne women were considered by white Americans to be attractive, and by Indian culture to be remarkably virtuous. The Arapaho did not seem to bear any of these "burdens."

The Cheyenne and the Arapaho both practiced the Sun Dance ritual and were the primary promoters of the ceremony, along with the Oglala tribe of the Teton Sioux. Some twenty-six tribes performed one version or another of the Sun Dance, but none as completely, with the attendant self-torture, as these three tribes. (The details of the Sun Dance are discussed in the section

Chief Dull Knife, the Cheyenne leader who organized a disastrous escape attempt from Fort Robinson in 1879.

Various tribes attempted to negotiate with the U.S. government, often to no purpose. The delegation of Cheyenne and Arapaho chiefs shown above was led by Black Kettle (center, standing) and Little Raven (seated, second from left).

dealing with the Teton Sioux, because the ritual is most closely associated with that Indian nation.)

Largely because of the raids by the Dakota Sioux, both nations migrated across the Missouri and into the upper Platte River Valley. From strictly agricultural cultures, they transformed into nomadic, buffalo-hunting peoples and became an important part of the Plains Indians with striking speed. Their new lives put them in close contact, and thus in conflict, with a new set of foes: the Sioux in the north and the Kiowa, Comanche, and Apache in the south. In the 1830s, this split the two nations into Northern and Southern Cheyenne and Arapaho. The northern groups settled the Wyoming area, and the southern groups settled the Colorado area.

The Cheyenne and Arapaho, probably because they had been displaced and forced to adopt a whole new way of life,

were very sensitive about their territorial sovereignty. From the first, they resented the "invasion" of settlers looking to establish themselves on Indian land or making their way to the California or Oregon coast. The tensions eased with the signing of the Fort Laramie Treaty in 1851, but the 1854 discovery of gold in the Black Hills (in Northern Cheyenne territory) and the 1861 runs to settle Nebraska and Kansas (in Southern Cheyenne territory), compromised these agreements and created a volatile environment. The U.S. Army attempted to circumvent the original treaty by coercing a few southern chiefs to sign the Fort Wise Treaty of 1861. Under the terms of this treaty, the Cheyenne and Arapaho renounced claims to their land in return for safe conduct to a small reservation in southeastern Colorado. The Northern Cheyenne and Arapaho repudiated this treaty, as did most of the southern members of these tribes.

The result was the bloody Cheyenne and Arapaho War of 1864–65, in which atrocities were committed by both sides. The so-called Dog Soldiers of the Cheyenne—their elite warriors—showed themselves to be a formidable force during the 1860s under the leadership of Tall Bull. The key event in the war was the Sand Creek Massacre of 1864, in which a unit of Colorado volunteers commanded by Colonel John M. Chivington attacked a Cheyenne village that had been guaranteed safety, and slaughtered and mutilated one hundred and fifty men, women, and children. Chief Black Kettle had tried for some time to make peace between his people and the United States by restraining his braves from seeking vengeance for raids and massacres that would have angered lesser men. It is possible that Chivington was directed to attack Black Kettle's villages by Colorado governor John Evans to provoke the chief and thus to quell eastern criticisms of the Government's Indian policy. If this was the intent, it both succeeded and failed: the public reaction was outrage, but Black Kettle, who just managed to escape with his life, capitulated and signed the Treaty of Little Arkansas that ended the war.

The American government realized that a new policy for the Plains Indians was going to be necessary, not only to allow communication, rail lines, and wagon trains of westward-bound settlers to pass through Indian territory but also to allow for the eventual settling of the land by whites. The result was the Medicine Lodge Treaty of 1867, a document that spelled the end of Indian civilization on the Great Plains and perhaps on the entire continent, because it bound all other Indian nations, even though only the Cheyenne and Arapaho were represented. (This was in keeping with government attitudes that lumped all Indian tribes into one category.) The members of the U.S. Peace Commission who negotiated

A delegation of Sioux and Cheyenne at a meeting in Fort Laramie, Wyoming, in 1868. Roman Nose is seated, second from left. The chiefs, who were practiced tacticians, were well aware of the military power of the U.S. Army and sued for peace at every opportunity.

the treaty were well aware of its implications but never bothered to explain them to the Indians. This time the prestige of Chief Black Kettle was not enough to prevent bloodshed.

Tall Bull organized his Dog Soldiers and pledged his allegiance to a new leader, Roman Nose. Roman Nose was actually a medicine man (the chiefdom of an Indian tribe was not assumable by anyone while

The Battle of Beecher's Island, September 17–25, 1868.

the chief was alive) who believed that his war bonnet had magical properties that protected him in battle. Roman Nose met with the Peace Commission at Medicine Lodge and saw through the intentions of the U.S. negotiators. He refused to sign the treaty and left to form a new fighting force that included the Sioux and the Cheyenne Dog Soldiers. This force was responsible

for the defeat of the small group of scouts commanded by Major George Forsyth at the Battle of Beecher's Island, which took place between September 17 and 25, 1868, on an island in the Arickaree Fork of the Republican River in Colorado. The island was named after a Lieutenant F.A. Beecher, who held out with a few men before succumbing to the charge of the Indians. The battle also took its toll on the Cheyenne because Roman Nose was killed on the first day of the battle; in fact, he had had a premonition the night before that the magic was gone from his war bonnet and that he would die in battle.

The Southern Cheyenne bore the brunt of the U.S. Army's campaign against the Indians, with Tall Bull leading the combined forces of Cheyenne, Arapaho, and Sioux warriors. Tall Bull himself was killed at the Battle of Summit Springs in Colorado on July 11, 1869, and the Dog Soldiers were left without a strong leader to take them into battle. The Southern Cheyenne refused to abandon the Plains and accept the reservation until they were decisively defeated in the Red River War of 1874. The Arapaho, who depended on the Cheyenne for their military muscle, suddenly became defenseless, and much of the vengeful anger felt by the soldiers and the government was directed at them.

Meanwhile, the Northern Cheyenne, led by Chief Dull Knife, had better results in their battle against the U.S. Army, mainly because they had the support of their old nemesis, the Sioux. Cheyenne warriors seemed to make up only a small portion of the attacking force at the Battle of the Rosebud and the Battle of the Little Big Horn, both of which resulted in decisive Indian victories. But the end of the Cheyenne's military resistance was at hand. In 1876 General Ranald Mackenzie dealt a decisive blow in a surprise attack on their winter encampment at the Powder River. By September 1878 Dull Knife's camp in Oklahoma's Indian Territory was weakened by hunger and disease; it was clear to the Cheyenne that the only way the tribe would survive was to return to its hunting grounds in Montana to the north.

Dull Knife announced that he was leading his people back to their ancestral home in Minnesota, and although he made it clear that his intentions were peaceful, the countryside prepared for a violent confrontation in what became known as Dull Knife's Raid. After crossing the Platte, the party divided into two groups. Dull Knife led his group to Fort Robinson, noisily proclaiming his intention to surrender, hoping that the second, smaller group, led by Little Wolf, might make it to Montana. (When he marched into Fort Robinson, the band seemed to be without weapons; the soldiers did not realize that the Cheyenne had dismantled their guns and turned them into jewelry and common utensils.)

For a time, the ruse seemed to work, though Dull Knife could hardly have expected the brutal treatment he and his people received at Fort Robinson. But in 1879 Little Wolf was contacted by his friend, Captain W.P. Clark, who convinced the chief to surrender. In January 1879 the Cheyenne prisoners at Fort Robinson reassembled their guns, and Dull Knife led a desperate escape attempt in which a third of his entire party, including members of his family, was slain. Dull Knife himself escaped and was taken in by the Sioux until his death in 1883. He was buried on a bluff on the banks of the Rosebud River, within sight of the land to which he had hoped to lead his people.

Geronimo (left) and Natchez at Fort Bowie, Arizona, after their surrender to General Miles in 1886.

THE EASTERN SIOUX:

LITTLE CROW AND THE MINNESOTA UPRISING

The tribe that was the most numerous, the most feared, and the most respected by their military adversaries of all the various Indians of the West were the Sioux of the Great Plains. The name is a variation of the Algonquin word for "enemy"—the Sioux called themselves the Dakota (or Lakota, or Nakota, depending on the dialect), which means "allies." Both terms were apt, because the Sioux had a very strong sense of solidarity that made them formidable foes to all other Indian tribes and to the white Americans in the process of settling the West.

The Sioux consisted of three main groups: the Eastern, or Santee, Sioux; the Central, or Yankton, Sioux; and the Western, or Teton, Sioux. Each of these groups was further divided into different

subtribes (more than clans, because each had a distinctive dialect of the Sioux language). The subtribe with the largest population was the Oglala of the Teton Sioux, and they had the greatest influence of any Sioux on the history of the West. The Sioux had a rich cultural and folk tradition. The stereotypical image that white America has of the proud Indian man wearing a full eagle-feather headdress, tall and strong with high cheekbones and a full nose, is an image of the Sioux. The Sioux were excellent fighters who organized their warriors into divisions and exercised the ordinary cautions one associates with advanced military science. It was the Sioux who used the teepee in large settlements across the plains.

The Sioux made it clear to settlers passing through that they objected to white intrusion onto their land, and their great numbers made any thought of ignoring these warnings virtually suicidal. Until after the Civil War, the approach of the U.S. government to the Sioux was cordial and respectful. White settlers did not cross Sioux lands or build settlements on them without a formal agreement being worked out between the United States and the tribe occupying the land. After the Civil War, the influx of Americans became a problem in

The Minnesota Valley was an area that was considered both valuable and sacred by the Sioux, and settling this area proved particularly difficult. In this 1893 depiction, settlers are being driven out of their homes.

Contrary to popular notions, scalping was practiced as much by European settlers against Indians (as proof of having killed an Indian, to collect a reward) as by Indians against Europeans. This 1873 cartoon appeared under the title "Which is the Savage?" and was part of a widespread effort by many easterners to change U.S. policy toward Native Americans.

Minnesota, where settlers took liberties with the land that were clearly not contained in the original treaties.

The leader of the Santee Sioux at this time was Chief Little Crow (although it seems the Santee chief had been called Little Crow for generations—his Sioux name was *Taoya-Teduta*, which means "Red People"). He was a puzzling figure in the history of the West. On the one hand, Little Crow was a dignified, proud Sioux chief, bearer of a great name and tradition. On the other hand, he reportedly converted to Christianity and was a member of a church near Fort Ridgely, Minnesota, and he showed great deference to whites and to the U.S. government. With tensions rising in

Minnesota, he traveled to Washington in 1858 and was dismayed to discover that the Indian commissioner, Charles Mix, demanded that the Sioux relinquish even more land and confine themselves to a small reservation along the Minnesota River. Little Crow reluctantly signed the treaty but felt he had made an honorable deal with the commissioner because the treaty guaranteed that the Indians would be supplied with food and other goods by the U.S. government.

During the summer of 1862, the shipment of food was delayed. Facing starvation, the Sioux became very agitated and the situation grew extremely tense. The result was the Minnesota Uprising of 1862, in which more than a thousand white settlers were killed—it was the largest killing action against whites by Indians in the history of the American West. It was said that Little Crow had originally attempted to dissuade his people from warring with the whites, but once he saw he would be overruled, he led the uprising with vigor. He had wanted to launch an attack on Fort Ridgely before it could be reinforced, but younger braves insisted on concentrating their attacks on the town of New Ulm. It turned out that Little Crow had had the right idea; by the time the Sioux turned their attention to the fort, it had been reinforced with infantry and cannon, which meant the ultimate defeat of the Sioux. The reprisals the U.S. Army made against the Santee were harsh; many of the Sioux leaders were tried as common criminals in civil courts and hanged, even though they could claim to have been soldiers at war.

In 1863 the Sioux were driven out of Minnesota and took refuge with the Yankton Sioux to the south. Little Crow and his son were shot while picking berries in July 1863; his scalp was displayed as a trophy for many years by the Minnesota State Historical Society.

THE TETON SIOUX:

CRAZY HORSE, RED CLOUD, GALL, AND SITTING BULL

The reconstituted Sioux nation settled into the area bounded by the Platte River Valley, the Upper Missouri and Yellowstone rivers, and the eastern Rocky Mountains. They became the core of the Indians of the Great Plains and had very little contact with the white world. However, the Teton Sioux, and especially the Oglala, fascinated the whites who studied Indians in the nineteenth century. The Oglala clearly had a well-developed culture that looked at the world in totally different terms from Europeans yet with an internal logic and a compelling worldview. Perhaps nowhere in Indian culture was this more apparent than in the Sun Dance ritual. The idea behind the Sun Dance was not, as many have supposed, worship of the sun; in fact, a more precise translation of the Indian name for the ritual would be "sun-gazing dance."

The warrior who underwent the Sun Dance hoped to inspire pity on the part of the Great Spirit (sometimes said to reside in the sun), so that the sufferer, and hence his tribe, would be worthy of the good that had happened or was going to happen to him. The participant proved by his sacrifice his unwavering and unequivocal devotion to the tribe; it would indeed be difficult to question the loyalty of anyone who went through the Sun Dance.

The ceremony was performed only by men, although the entire tribe was invited to watch and provide chanting and encour-

Sitting Bull (1834–1890), after a photograph taken in 1885.

agement. Shamans or men who had already undergone the ceremony supervised and led the chanting, as well as the vows and burning of incense. They also concocted and administered drugs (which the participants certainly required). The ceremony itself began with a vow taken by the participants that they were undergoing the ritual for the benefit of their people. The shamans led processions from one portion of the

Right: Native American religions often preached an integration of human and natural forces, as in the way body markings symbolize the layers formed by the forces that created stratified layers of rock or tree rings. Below: The most ecstatic and intense Native American religious ceremony known to Europeans was the Sun Dance, a ceremony that tried to unlock and harness the power of physical pain.

ceremony to the next—from the selection of sacred trees to be fashioned into poles to the harvesting of the ingredients for the elixirs used to paint the bodies of the dancers—heightening the tribe's ecstasy at each stage.

The poles were then erected, sometimes with crossbars between them, inside a tent specially raised for the ceremony. Meaningful objects from the tribe's history, religion, or lore, including the scalps of defeated enemies, were placed on the poles. The ceremony was a weeklong affair, with the dancers prepared for the ordeal during the first three days. Their bodies were painted white and then painted with symbols. They donned loincloths, anklets, wristbands, and headbands, all sanctified by the medicine men. During the preparatory days, they fasted, not even drinking water, but ingesting drugs that induced intoxication and ecstasy. They were then ready for the finale. Skewers were passed

through the skin and muscle of their chests and backs. The skewers were attached to leather straps and then to weights that dangled and pulled on the skin. On the final day—when the combination of pain and drugs had induced in the dancer a near-psychotic state—the leather straps were attached to the top of the sacred poles or the crossbars, and each "dancer" was suspended, held aloft by the skewers dug into his flesh. The pain from this phase of the ceremony was nearly always great enough to cause the dancer, however drugged, to lose consciousness. Finally, the ceremony ended with the dancers being cut down as the sun rose on the last day. A dancer would often recall visions he had during the dance and relate them to the tribe—these would then enter the tribal lore.

White men, and even Indians who were not members of the tribe, were not permitted to witness the Sun Dance. In fact, for many years white scholars and settlers who heard stories about the ceremony believed it was wholly fictitious (and pointed to it as proof of the untrustworthiness of the Indians). Warriors who underwent the Sun Dance were ministered to afterward so as to accentuate their wounds, which were displayed as a badge of honor, but white observers attributed these wounds to battle scars. After years of patient and often dangerous investigation, anthropologists verified the truth of the ceremony. (The sum of this research was collected by Clark Wissler and published by the American Museum of Natural History in 1921.)

The Sun Dance was banned by the federal government in 1904, ostensibly (and ironically) because it represented inhuman cruelty. But the government's real motive—as the suppression of the Ghost Dance religion indicates—was to curtail any Indian activities that could cause a resurgence of Indian nationalism. The Sun Dance ceremony

An Indian warrior forbidding the passage of a wagon train through his territory. The spear in the ground and his standing on his horse express emphasis.

survived in abbreviated and disguised form, often as Fourth of July celebrations, well into the twentieth century.

The ceremony was vividly portrayed in the 1970 film *A Man Called Horse*, in which Richard Harris portrays a white man who is captured by the Sioux and allowed to enter the tribe only after undergoing the Sun Dance ritual. The ceremony was depicted in the film (and reprised in its two sequels) with close attention to detail, but, in fact, the use of the ceremony as an initiation into the tribe was a fanciful idea without any basis in fact.

As contact with pioneers and other whites increased, tensions mounted and the Sioux saw the potential for a repeat of the debacle that had driven some of their brethren out of Minnesota. In 1851 the U.S. government convinced several Sioux chiefs that peace could be maintained if the Indians would stay clear of certain trails and stations. The government promised to pay annuities to the Indians in return for compliance and also to take special pains to keep settlers off Indian territories, especially the buffalo hunting grounds. These agreements were incorporated into the Fort Laramie Treaty (also known as the Horse

The U.S. Cavalry was the primary instrument of U.S. policy toward the Indians. This regiment is stationed at Fort Laramie, Wyoming.

the Sioux was well known because when he discovered he had taken another man's cow, he offered many horses as restitution, but the Mormons would not be placated.

In command of the soldiers was a young second lieutenant, John L. Grattan, just a year out of West Point and eager to prove himself against the Sioux. He marched into the Sioux camp and set up a battle line in the middle of the camp. The Sioux finally realized that the soldiers had not come to take the horses they had offered and the chief, Conquering Bear, pleaded with the soldiers not to open fire. Accompanying the soldiers was an interpreter, who, it was later determined, was stone drunk during the entire episode. He garbled the words of both parties in translation—changing, for example, "we beseech you with words that come from our hearts" to "we will take you prisoner and eat your hearts"—and it was not long before Grattan fired his cannon at the chief at point-blank range, killing him. The inexperienced Grattan probably never realized how large an encampment he had ridden into, but when the first shots rang out, it took the Sioux only a few minutes to overrun the soldiers and kill all of them.

Older chiefs prevailed on the younger warriors not to obliterate Fort Laramie itself, which at the time had only about fifty soldiers. They explained the circumstances to Fleming, whose report to the agent was sympathetic to the Sioux. The agent's official report placed blame squarely on Grattan's shoulders, but public and official opinion back east demanded that reprisals be taken. A year later, General William Selby Harney—fresh from his victories against Mexico—left Fort Leavenworth, Kansas, with a force of seven hundred cavalry, fully equipped with cannon. This group conducted several killing raids on Sioux villages, resulting in the death of hundreds of

Creek Treaty) of 1851. Not all of the Sioux had agreed to the Fort Laramie treaty, however, so that when whites violated the terms (as happened soon and often), the Sioux who had not been signators reacted violently, which outraged the federal authorities back in Washington and Americans in the East generally.

One incident that had long-lasting repercussions was the Grattan Massacre of 1854. It began when a cow wandered from a Mormon wagon train passing through Sioux territory and was killed and eaten by a Sioux tribe, who thought it was an overdue payment from the Indian agent. The Mormons complained to Lieutenant Hugh Fleming, the commander at Fort Laramie, who was not inclined to do anything until the Indian agent arrived. He sent a unit of twenty-six men, equipped with two cannon, to the Sioux camp to arrest the Indian who had taken the cow. The identity of

men, women, and children. Harney finally met with Sioux leaders and Indian Agent Thomas Twiss in 1856 and became convinced that Grattan had foolishly brought about his own death.

The Fort Laramie Treaty was reaffirmed, and Harney dealt with the Sioux and the settlers with equal harshness. He substantiated the federal government's authority over the western lands by leading cavalry units and crossing through hunting grounds and sacred areas of the Sioux at will. Yet at the same time, Harney enforced the terms of the treaty and brooked no opposition from the pioneers passing through or from the settlers trying to establish themselves in the area. He was especially stern with the Mormons, who did not accept federal authority in the first place. Harney was on his way to arrest and hang Brigham Young for treason (and would certainly have done so) when he was sent to Oregon to deal with the British. Between 1856 and 1863, the area inhabited by the Sioux was fairly peaceful under Harney's authority. He retired in 1863 when he was not given a command in the Union Army because he was suspected of being sympathetic to the Confederate cause.

After Harney, the administration of the Western Division became lax and the constant encroachment of white settlers and hunters on the buffalo herds made conflict inevitable. Between 1864 and 1876, the U.S. government pursued what it called a Peace Policy, aimed at pacifying the Sioux, mollifying them with bribes and gifts, and promising them enforcement of the borders of their territories. The Indian Bureau clearly believed that this would provide them an opportunity to turn the "savages" into Christians and assimilate them into white European society. This approach would have been doomed even if the terms of the agreements with the Sioux had been upheld, but that was not the case. Several incidents pitted the Sioux against settler groups or the U.S. Cavalry—some, like the Sand Creek Massacre of 1864, ended disastrously for the Indians; others, like the Fetterman Massacre of 1866, ended disastrously for the whites; but most, like the Wagon-Box Fight of 1867, ended in a draw. These skirmishes accomplished nothing except an increase in tensions. The discovery of gold in the Black Hills in the 1870s, with the attendant influx of miners and settlers who could not have been less interested in any prior agreement with the Sioux, resulted in the Sioux War of 1876.

The inscription at the bottom of this photograph reads, "Red Cloud and American Horse, the two most noted Chiefs now living. Photo and Copyright 1891 by Grabill... Deadwood, S.D."

Red Cloud, chief of the Sioux.

Red Cloud himself was a controversial leader of the Sioux, sometimes battling the U.S. Cavalry successfully—he is said to have been the only Indian chief to win a war against the United States—and sometimes capitulating, in the eyes of many Sioux, to promote his own fortunes. He was born in 1822 and given the Indian name *Makhpiya-Luta*, which means "Red Sky," a reference to a meteor that reddened the sky around the time of his birth. Red Cloud became a chief of a small portion of the Oglala as a result of his assassination of Bull Bear, chief of the larger segment of the Oglala, and a rival of his uncle Smoke. The assassination split the Oglala for many decades and made Red Cloud an ineffectual leader of the Sioux. Yet it was largely the forces led by Red Cloud and commanded by Crazy Horse that challenged the U.S. plan to open the Bozeman Trail. The U.S. government considered Red Cloud to be leader of all the Sioux because of his leadership in the Fetterman Massacre. When the army finally withdrew, burning down the Powder River forts built along the Bozeman Trail, Red Cloud's prestige rose among the Sioux, although he was not accepted by all the clans or even seen as a legitimate chief by most Sioux.

It was during this war that several great Sioux leaders emerged to become legends for the Sioux people and for students of military leadership. One of the earliest great chiefs was Crazy Horse, an Oglala whose marriage to a Cheyenne woman cemented relations between the two nations. Crazy Horse was born in 1841, and his Indian name was *Tashunca-uitco*, which translates more accurately as "He whose horse is crazy," an allusion to the wild abandon with which he attacked an enemy in battle. Crazy Horse participated in both the Fetterman Massacre and the Wagon-Box Fight, leading the forces loyal to Chief Red Cloud. Crazy Horse remained a follower of Red Cloud until the chief seemed to bow to the will of the whites.

In 1870 Red Cloud traveled to New York and Washington, where he was treated like a visiting potentate. He may well have thought that the support of Washington would enlarge his rule over his own people, but when he returned, he had made so many concessions to the United States and had gained so many personal advantages (not the least of which was being afforded a residence at the Indian Bureau post) that he lost the respect of his people. From this point on, Red Cloud became a figure trusted by neither side, so he was of little help when the Sioux rejected the Fort Laramie Treaty, or during the crisis caused by the Black Hills gold strike, or during the suppression of the Ghost Dance religion in 1890. Red Cloud tried to maintain Sioux customs and traditions but usually within the context of the white society and under U.S. protection. Some Sioux looked upon this as the beginning of the "museumification" of Indian culture and looked elsewhere for leadership as long as the Sioux were a viable independent unit.

With Red Cloud out of the picture, Crazy Horse looked for another mentor and joined Sitting Bull in his ongoing battle with the cavalry. Crazy Horse was one of Sitting Bull's two lieutenants in the campaign against Custer and Crook in the Yellow River campaigns of 1872–73. The other lieutenant was Gall (or *Pizi* in Sioux), a chief of the smaller Hunkpapa Sioux. Gall seems to have been in command of the Sioux warriors who kept Major Reno pinned down during the Battle of Little Big Horn, allowing Crazy Horse to lead his soldiers against Custer's column. Both Crazy Horse and Gall fled with Sitting Bull to Canada after the defeat of Custer. Crazy Horse remained devoted to Sitting Bull and continued a guerrilla campaign against the U.S. Army led by Nelson Miles. But Gall had a falling-out with Sitting Bull and returned to the United States and surrendered—later on the calendar than Crazy Horse, although his opposition to the United States had in fact ended earlier. Gall became a judge on the Court of Indian Offenses and gained celebrity in Washington as an authentic Sioux chief who nonetheless sought to have

A delegation of Oglala Sioux chiefs, with peace pipes in hand, for a council with cavalry officers. Red Cloud is seated in the center; interpreter John Bridgeman is standing behind him.

his tribe's children educated in the ways of American and western culture.

Gall and Red Cloud, and their families and allies, lived protected lives, supported by the U.S. Department of the Interior, and were paraded out whenever it was necessary to support government action against an attempt by the Indians at self-determination. They opposed Sitting Bull and Wovoka and campaigned actively among their people against the Ghost Dance religion. Gall died in 1894 and Red Cloud in 1909, well after the tragedy of the Wounded Knee Massacre.

Crazy Horse finally surrendered to the United States on May 6, 1877, and agreed to settle on the reservation. To prove his acceptance of the new arrangement, he was asked to help the United States track and catch up to the Nez Percé, who had left their reservation in Oregon and were fleeing to Canada. The scout who served as translator, Frank Grouard, was an old enemy of Crazy Horse and deliberately mistranslated the chief's reply, leading the soldiers in Fort Robinson to conclude that Crazy Horse was inspired by the Nez Percé to lead his people off the reservation. In fact, he was telling the authorities that he would help them after he had taken his sick wife back to her father's house among the Cheyenne. When he returned from taking his wife home to her people—without the authorization he thought Grouard had arranged—he was arrested and stabbed to death in the ensuing scuffle.

This left only one Sioux Chief—Sitting Bull—who could lead the Sioux nation in an uncompromising quest for nationhood and cultural independence. Sitting Bull was born *Tatanka Iyotake* (which means "Sitting Bull") in 1831 in what is now South Dakota. He distinguished himself as a brave warrior in his youth and believed that he was gifted with a vision for himself and his people.

Above: Chief Gall of the Hunkpapa Sioux, one of the military leaders of the attack on Custer's troops at the Little Big Horn in 1876. Opposite: A rare photo of Sitting Bull in full costume, taken in 1884.

Sitting Bull was a deeply religious man who saw himself as connected to all living beings and to the cosmos in a manner reminiscent of eastern mystics. As a member of the Hunkpapa tribe, he had little contact with whites during the 1840s and 1850s. At that time, he was more involved in warring against other Indian nations for hunting privileges in the Yellowstone and Powder river valleys.

Sitting Bull seemed to be antagonistic to whites from an early age, not because of any specific incident, but because of his fierce sense of Sioux identity and his hopes for his people. He was not involved in the

Minnesota Uprising or the Red Cloud War and did not even look upon whites as serious adversaries until after Red Cloud's capitulation in 1868. In turn, whites never regarded Sitting Bull as anything other than a medicine man who was concerned with the spiritual values of the Sioux rather than with the political realities of land and boundaries. Whites took almost no note of Sitting Bull's designation as spiritual chief of an amalgamation of those Sioux tribes not inclined to follow Red Cloud. This was a position previously unknown in Sioux society. It was the first time Indian tribes had formed an ongoing association that was more enduring than a momentary military alliance.

Once the Sioux made this breakthrough, Sitting Bull devoted his energy to creating a unified and disciplined fighting force out of the disparate clans and tribes. In June 1876, to signify his becoming chief of the Sioux nation, he underwent the Sun Dance ritual at the advanced age of forty-five. It is said that Sitting Bull had a vision of the defeat of Custer during the ritual. In the ensuing weeks, the Sioux, led by Sitting Bull and under the military command of Crazy Horse and Gall, scored stunning victories— Crook at the Rosebud and Custer at the Little Big Horn. In the aftermath of these victories, however, the Indians were not adept at following through. For reasons that are still not clear, Sitting Bull was not able to use his advantageous position to force the U.S. government into granting the Sioux better and more secure borders. Instead, the Sioux scattered into the Black

The Indian Wars were settled in councils like this one held at Pine Ridge South Dakota. The agreements forged at these meetings were broken again and again by the U.S. government, which believed no contract with a Native American was binding.

Hills and toward the Rockies, losing the power of their numbers. Sitting Bull and his immediate followers fled to Canada, though the Canadian government would not guarantee their safety or take responsibility for their sustenance. Many of Sitting Bull's followers became disenchanted and returned to the United States, in some cases to be imprisoned or taken in shackles to the reservation.

Sitting Bull returned to the United States and surrendered at Fort Buford on July 19, 1881, and after a short period in prison, he was brought to the reservation. In 1885 he traveled with Buffalo Bill's Wild West Show, but he was clearly contemptuous of the American society that he observed on tour and did not come back for a second season. Throughout his life,

Sitting Bull was a voice against the abridgement of Sioux land and rights, and for the maintenance of the Sioux language, culture, and traditions. When Indian discontent with the reservation gave rise to the Ghost Dance crisis of 1890, Indian Agent James McLaughlin, a longtime enemy of Sitting Bull, feared that the chief's support of Wovoka would bring on a full-scale Indian uprising. On the pretext of wishing to place Sitting Bull in protective custody, McLaughlin sent Indian police to the chief's cabin on the Grand River on December 15, 1890. What transpired there has been the subject of controversy for many years, but the result was that Sitting Bull was shot dead by Red Tomahawk and Bull Head, and thirteen others from both sides died in the shoot-out.

A remarkable sequence: George Catlin's sketch of himself painting a Crow Chief (right), and the finished painting of the chief in full profile and in regalia (below).

THE SHOSHONE AND THE COMANCHE:

CHIEF WASHAKIE AND QUANAH PARKER

Two Indian nations with intertwined histories are the Shoshone and their offshoot, the Comanche. Both nations were physically different from their neighbors, the Sioux, and many other tribes. They were generally short and stocky, and not nearly as athletic as other tribes. Both tribes, however, were unparalleled horseriders. George Catlin, the artist who lived among the Indians and painted them, waxed poetic in describing the horsemanship of the Shoshone and the Comanche. And anthropologists have come to believe that this talent (as well as their physical attributes) indicate that their ancestry may have been in the Mongolian steppes.

The Shoshone showed an initial friendliness to the first white explorers who came into the West. Sacajawea, the Indian woman who served as a guide to Lewis and Clark in their 1804–06 expedition, was a member of the Shoshone tribe. The early pioneers who passed through Shoshone territory—nestled against the eastern slopes of the Rocky Mountains in western Wyoming—must have impressed them as strictly farmers, and the Shoshone extended to them every assistance (of course, in getting through and out of their territory). The Shoshone were able to scratch out a living in inhospitable areas, which caused them to be known as Digger Indians. In 1781 the Shoshone were stricken with an epidemic of smallpox that greatly reduced the tribe's population, especially in the north. They were in the middle of a protracted war with the Blackfoot, and the combination of disease and war drove the tribe out of the Montana plains. The Blackfoot suffered their own, even worse smallpox epidemic in 1837, with the result that the Shoshone were geographically isolated and free from the threat of warring tribes or encroaching whites.

In 1843 the wagon trains passing through Shoshone territory began to encounter resistance from the tribe; many journals indicate that the sight of Shoshone riders, dressed ordinarily in striking Indian regalia, had an unsettling effect on the pioneers, and panicky potshots were often taken at scouts merely monitoring the train's progress. The Shoshone made it clear that they would not tolerate wagon trains on their land, and several whole trains (including a Mormon encampment at Fort Lemhiwere) were wiped out by the tribe.

Between 1863 and 1868, a series of battles between the Shoshone and a force of white volunteers led by Colonel Patrick Connor made it clear to the Indians that a peace with the United States was in their best interest. A reservation was created near Fort Hall in exchange for guarantees of safe passage on the trails to the Northwest.

A group of Shoshone in central Wyoming around the Wind River region were sheltered from these conflicts but recognized early the futility of fighting the U.S. Cavalry. Under the leadership of Chief Washakie, the Wind River Shoshone became a friend to the wagon trains and a valuable ally of the cavalry. Chief Washakie was a celebrated warrior and a talented administrator, though he ruled his people with an iron hand—in a fit of anger, he once shot a brave dead for challenging him. Washakie probably realized better than other chiefs the importance

of the treaty in the white man's world, and he took pains to negotiate terms that would be hard to break. In addition, he was able to offer the cavalry valuable assistance in the war against the Sioux through scouting and sharing knowledge of the terrain. Washakie was more than happy to help the United States vanquish his tribe's traditional enemies, but he made certain that his tribe received payment or concessions in exchange for their help.

Washakie died in 1900, but in the early years of the twentieth century, the Shoshone showed that they had learned their lesson

well from the old chief. They had a firm sense of the value of their reservation lands and were able to negotiate terms favorable to the tribe. Other Indian tribes regarded the Wind River Shoshone as in league with the devil white man and have accused the tribe of betraying their Indian heritage. But the Shoshone recognized no such solidarity—and in fact none existed. The tribes of North America were never confederated and had always regarded each other as real or potential enemies. The Shoshone had fared worse than most

Sacajawea guiding Lewis and Clark through the wilderness. Without her help, it is doubtful the pair would have ever made it back from their expedition.

Native American buffalo hunters continued hunting buffalo by bow and arrow in a time-honored tradition even after they had firearms at their disposal.

nations at the hands of other tribes and felt no kinship with them in their conflict with the whites.

The Comanche were an offshoot of the Shoshone tribe. The Comanche were regarded across the plains as excellent horsemen, and unlike the Shoshone, the area they inhabited in the southwestern plains would be of interest only to people adept at hunting buffalo. The Comanche were unequaled in this and could very well have subsisted on the buffalo herds indefinitely. The buffalo—the purely American name for the North American bison—is a remarkably hardy animal that has few natural enemies. They proliferated over the

prairie because of their ability to climb and swim to new grazing areas. The buffalo's strength, as well as its regal bearing, led the Indians to believe that the animal was a godly (or, more properly, god-owned) creature. The Comanche, therefore, worshipped and respected the buffalo even while they hunted them and depended on them for food and hides.

The degree to which the white buffalo hunters (supported, protected, and encouraged by the U.S. government) decimated the herds and nearly caused the extinction of the animal is unequivocally proven by the numbers: in 1800 an estimated sixty million buffalo roamed the American prairie;

by 1870 that number was down to about five million; in 1900 only an estimated three hundred buffalo were to be found on the continent. The Comanche rightly determined that the unchecked hunting of the buffalo was an attempt to deprive them of their food source. To put these numbers in perspective, the Comanche, who hunted buffalo for food, using hides only of animals eaten, required no more than 75,000 animals a year to meet all their needs. The Comanche waged a bloody campaign against any group who challenged either them or their herds, including the Spanish, the Mexicans, the Texans, and the Apache. The Comanche believed that some of the smallpox epidemics that had been suffered by other tribes had been deliberately introduced by white traders, so they were alert to any possible treachery by whites, and sometimes massacred trading posts if they suspected the settlers of trying to introduce disease in their midst.

In 1836 the Comanche captured a nine-year-old girl named Cynthia Ann Parker during a raid on a trading post near Waco, Texas. Four other children were taken, but two were rescued and two others were ransomed; only Cynthia remained with the Comanche. The girl was raised as a Comanche and eventually became the wife of a chief, Nocona, bearing him three children. The eldest, an uncharacteristically tall boy named Quanah, became a warrior in the Kwahadi band, the elite fighters of the Comanche. In time, Quanah, who identified himself as pure Comanche although he was physically an anomaly in the tribe, became chief of the Comanche and waged war on

Left: Cynthia Ann Parker, the mother of Quanah Parker, in 1860, shortly after her recapture by Texas Rangers. Below: Approximately forty thousand buffalo hides piled high in Rath and Wright's fur yards in Dodge City, Kansas, in 1878.

Two views of Comanche chief Quanah Parker: on horseback in full chief's headdress (above); and as a medicine man (right).

those he considered to be the real enemy of the Comanche: the buffalo hunters.

The buffalo hunters conducted a brisk trade in buffalo hides out of a fort called Adobe Walls on the Canadian River in the Texas Panhandle. Two battles between the Comanche and the hunters, which became known as the battles of Adobe Walls, took place at this fort. The first battle took place in November 1864 and resulted in a rout of the Comanche. The hunters, led by the legendary scout Kit Carson, had several Howitzer cannons at their disposal and were able to establish command of the area for the next decade. The Comanche were pressured to sign the Medicine Lodge Treaty of 1867 but refused, taking to the plains and preparing themselves for a new assault under the leadership of their new chief—Quanah.

By the time Quanah became chief of the Comanche, the buffalo herd had been reduced to about a fifth of its original size, and the tribe knew that this put its very survival into question. A second attack on the fort took place on June 27, 1874. It was led by Quanah and involved a combined force of seven hundred Comanche, Arapaho, and Kiowa warriors. The hunters had, in the interim, built a new Adobe Walls fort with stronger fortifications and cannon enplacements. Again under the leadership of Carson, and with the assistance of such celebrated gunmen as Bat Masterson and Bill Dixon, some thirty hunters beat back the Comanche assault. The Sharp rifles that the hunters used on the buffalo—single-shot rifles with a powerful calibre and high accuracy—proved extremely effective against the attacking Indians. More than half of the attacking force fell, while only three of the hunters were killed. Quanah's horse was shot out from under him, and he just barely survived the battle.

The defeat of the Indians at the Second Battle of Adobe Walls spelled doom for the Comanche, and Quanah decided on a new approach (perhaps taking a page out of Chief Washakie's notebook). He surrendered formally to the U.S. Army in May 1875, declaring that the Comanche were giving up their nomadic life and adapting to the white man's society. He adopted the name Quanah Parker and settled with a large portion of the Comanche on a reservation in the Texas-Oklahoma panhandles. Soon Quanah Parker became the effective chief of the Comanche, Kiowa, and Apache, and he became a wealthy man as the eloquent (he was fluent in both English and Spanish) spokesman for the Indians. He encouraged education and agriculture among the Indians and promoted the assimilation of the Indian into American society but without rejecting Indian heritage and traditions. This was a fine line Quanah Parker had to walk, and not all the Comanche thought he did it well.

Quanah Parker never showed any interest in Christianity and was a regular user of mescal and peyote, creating a kind of religion based on the altered states induced by these drugs. He was also controversial among Americans because he was a polygamist—he openly married five women. His magnificent estate in Cache, Oklahoma, became a tourist attraction, and he became a celebrity, participating in the inauguration of Teddy Roosevelt in 1905. But many Indians viewed his approach as a wrongheaded betrayal of the Comanche people and its culture. He remained a controversial figure in the Indian community right up to his death in 1911.

And what happened to Cynthia Ann Parker? In 1860 the Parker family, who were then wealthy and powerful in Texas, arranged for a band of Texas Rangers and soldiers to "rescue" Cynthia Ann from the Comanche, along with her daughter, Topsannah. By then was in her thirties and was almost completely assimilated into Comanche culture. She tried to escape and return to the Comanche, but her family stopped her. A few years after her return to white society, Topsannah died, and Cynthia Ann fell into a deep depression. She starved herself to death in 1870. Quanah Parker's son, White Parker, would claim later that it was Cynthia Ann who had instilled in her son a love of white people and of American culture, which accounted for his willingness to assimilate into American society. By special act of Congress, Cynthia Ann and Quanah Parker were buried alongside one another in Oklahoma in 1911—in 1957, however, these graves were moved to make way for a missile testing range.

THE NEZ PERCÉ:

CHIEF JOSEPH

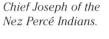

Chief Joseph of the Nez Percé Indians.

The Indian chief usually referred to as Chief Joseph is the son of the chief known as Old Chief Joseph, who was the leader of the Nez Percé Indians of the northwestern region of the United States until his death in 1871. The Nez Percé ("Pierced Nose") were named by early French fur trappers who encountered a different tribe of Indians, who did, indeed, pierce their noses to allow ornaments to be inserted. The Nez Percé, however, never pierced their noses, and they resented this name. The tribe obtained horses from the Shoshone in the early 1700s, and this enabled them to become excellent hunters who suddenly had access to the great buffalo herds. Over the course of the next century, the Nez Percé developed the Appaloosa, a speckled horse that was perfectly adapted to the hunt by virtue of its superior agility, stamina, and intelligence.

Old Chief Joseph was among the first to greet Lewis and Clark in the Pacific Northwest and offer peace and assistance to the explorers (although the allies of the Nez Percé, the Flathead, were not so hospitable). Old Chief Joseph (whose Indian name was *Tuekakas*) was converted to Christianity in 1836, baptized by the missionary Henry Spalding in 1838, and christened Joseph. The Nez Percé favored one particular area of the Pacific Northwest, the Wallowa Valley of Oregon. Old Chief Joseph made many concessions to the whites and put up with many indignities to vouchsafe that territory for his people. In 1855 the chief negotiated a treaty that placed the tribe on the Wallowa, greatly enhancing the chief's prestige among his people and with neighboring tribes.

It is easy to understand, then, the anger and disappointment that followed the sudden closing of the Wallowa reservation in 1863 and the order moving the entire Nez Percé nation to the Lapwai reservation in Idaho. (The primary reason for the move was that gold had been discovered in Oregon.) The old chief burned both his Bible and his American flag and urged his

The Nez Percé Indians were even more helpful than most Native Americans to European expansion. Here, they assist surveyors of the Missouri-Pacific Railroad in 1853.

people to resist the transfer to Idaho. The Nez Percé continued to hunt buffalo in Montana, while tensions between the tribe and the U.S. government increased. Old Chief Joseph died in 1871, and contrary to his desire to be buried in his beloved Wallowa Valley, he was buried near Lostine on the new reservation. In 1927 the old chief was reburied at the mouth of Wallowa Lake.

The tribe surprisingly chose the youngest of the old chief's sons to succeed his father; he was clearly the most intelligent of the three, and the Nez Percé realized that cunning was going to be an important weapon against the whites. The young chief, known as Chief Joseph, who was only thirty-one when he was elected, embarked on six difficult years of negotiations with the military commander of the area, General Oliver Otis Howard. The two men faced off at several meetings that were covered by the newspapers, which made Chief Joseph well known throughout the country. The chief refused to join the Sioux in their war against the U.S. Army, but in 1877, when

General Howard delivered an ultimatum to the Nez Percé that they either confine themselves to the reservation in Idaho or be forcibly taken there, the war councils of the tribe took control and the Nez Percé War broke out.

Chief Joseph's brother Olikut, eager to prove that the tribe had made a mistake in choosing his younger brother as chief, led the warriors of the tribe into several rash attacks, which inflicted heavy casualties on the cavalry but had little strategic value. When it became clear that the Nez Percé were no match for the U.S. Army, Chief Joseph took control, believing the tribe's only hope was to make a dash to Canada, just as Sitting Bull had after the Little Big Horn. The path to Canada was not an easy one, however, and the chief was not simply moving soldiers but the entire tribe. Many small battles were fought along the way, and many feints were tried in an effort to disguise the true destination of the tribe. But on October 5, 1877, in northern Minnesota, just thirty miles from the

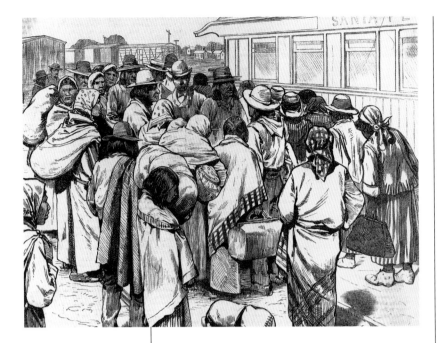

Canadian border, the tribe was surrounded by the cavalry, and Chief Joseph was forced to surrender to Colonel Nelson Miles.

Chief Joseph was able to maintain a quiet dignity even in the hour of defeat, and he became the symbol in many quarters of the "noble Indian," proud and devoted to the land. In time, an elaborate mythology grew around the chief in which great powers of diplomacy and military strategy were attributed to him; in truth, he was not respected by the tribe in military matters, and many of the diplomatic moves he made were dictated more by his inability to forge a consensus among the elders of the tribe than his own negotiating skill. After a period spent as prisoners at Fort Leavenworth, during which many died of malaria, the Nez Percé were moved to a reservation in Indian Territory in Oklahoma. They were surrounded by Indians hostile to them and exiled from their home in the Pacific Northwest. Chief Joseph died in 1904 and was buried on the Colville Reservation in northern Washington.

A number of stirring and captivating accounts of the life of Chief Joseph and the story of the Nez Percé have appeared in print, including Alvin M. Josephy's magisterial 1965 work, *Nez Percé Indians and the Opening of the Northwest*; Mark H. Brown's 1967 book, *The Flight of the Nez Percé*; and Merrill D. Beal's *I Will Fight No More Forever: Chief Joseph and the Nez Percé War*, published in 1963. The title of the Beal book refers to the final words of the classic and moving speech Chief Joseph uttered when he surrendered.

TAVIBO, WOVOKA, BIG FOOT,

AND THE GHOST DANCE

In the closing years of the nineteenth century, when the sun was setting on centuries of Indian life on the American continent, a phenomenon took place among the remaining tribes on the Great Plains that is still being studied today. It went under the name of the Ghost Dance religion, and it led to an incident that became emblematic of the history of the Indian on the frontier: the massacre at Wounded Knee. Anthropologists have been interested in the Ghost Dance phenomenon as an element of the death throes of a culture and have likened it to the imagery and beliefs of early Christians in the period before the destruction of the Israelite state at the hands of Rome.

Possibly the most amazing aspect of the Ghost Dance was how threatened white American society was by it. The Sioux nation and the various other peoples who adhered to and practiced the Ghost Dance were, by 1890, incapable of mounting any military action whatever. And the religion clearly had elements that rendered its adherents less capable of armed conflict. Yet the Ghost Dance gave rise to intense feelings among adherents, and it may have been the raw intensity of these emotions that frightened white America most. It was as if the Indians became aware of an element of their own psyche that would lead to a more developed and thus more powerful existence, and this was something white America could not brook.

The Ghost Dance religion had its origins in the Mason Valley area of Nevada. In 1870 a Paiute medicine man named Tavibo appeared on the scene, preaching to his people that a redemption of the Indian peoples was at hand. He issued several prophecies, some of which were very specific and some vague and general, but all of which conveyed a vision in which the Indian nations arose and reclaimed the land from the whites. His visions included images of the ground swallowing up the whites, and dead Indians rising from graves to take their place. He led ceremonies in which men, women, and children would dance in a circle for days at a time, chanting prayers and songs that, he claimed, had been revealed to him by the Great Spirit. It was called the Ghost Dance because Tavibo claimed to communicate with the dead during the trances he experienced while dancing.

Tavibo's name and teaching spread to many tribes in California and Oregon, but never found widespread acceptance in the Great Plains, especially when a number of the more precise prophecies made by Tavibo and his disciples did not come to pass. The sect might have disappeared with the death of Tavibo in the early 1870s, except that he left behind a talented student. This young man was about fifteen when Tavibo died, and he was raised in the area of Nevada where the Ghost Dance had its greatest impact. His name was Wovoka, but he was also known by the name Jack Wilson because he had lived with a Wilson family in his youth. Wovoka occasionally claimed to have been Tavibo's son, though these claims were made later on and usually when Wovoka was in a trance.

In 1889 an eclipse of the sun occurred in the Southwest, and Wovoka, who was suffering from a fever at the time, had a vision that he shared with his family and followers. In it, he had visited the Happy Hunting Ground where the Paiute ancestors were engaged in the kind of pursuits they had

The Native American spiritualist Wovoka (wearing the chief's feather in an armband, since federal law forbade it from being worn on the head).

The Ghost Dance, introduced by Wovoka, combined many aspects of Native American spiritualism without the use of the pain-inducing ceremonies of the Sun Dance.

tions of their dead relatives. Because of this, new teachings and prayers were frequently added to the religion. Often the dancers would dance in a circle until they fainted from exhaustion. The Sioux added a costume to the ritual: white "ghost shirts" on which were painted symbols of the sun, moon, and stars, and eagles or mythical creatures. The Sioux believed that these shirts turned the dancers into phantasmic creatures without corporeality, which, they believed, allowed them to communicate with the ghosts of the netherworld. They also had faith that the shirts made them impervious to arrows and bullets.

Wovoka found few converts in California, where the Indians remembered how Tavibo's prophecies had failed to come true, but the Ghost Dance spread quickly to the Plains Indians. By 1890 it was the dominant religion among the Sioux, Cheyenne, Comanche, Arapaho, and Shoshone, among others. The winter of 1890 was particularly brutal to the Indians on the reservation, and the news of Sitting Bull's death on December 15 created a sense of deep despair. The different families of the tribes turned to the Ghost Dance for consolation, and many groups tried to find areas where they could perform the ritual in private and apart from other groups. One group of Miniconjou Sioux moved off their usual camp on the reservation to an isolated area on the banks of Wounded Knee Creek on the Pine Ridge Reservation in South Dakota. On December 29, the Seventh Cavalry, under the command of Colonel James Forsyth, surrounded the camp and aimed their Hotchkiss rapid-fire guns at the tipis of the camp.

What precisely caused the soldiers to open fire is not clear. They were certainly in the process of searching the Indians for "hidden weapons," and it is possible that a few of the soldiers made lewd advances

been free to follow before the whites came. He had met the Great Spirit, he said, and was instructed how the Indians should dance and the prayers they should recite to rid themselves of the whites and bring back the olden times. He preached a message of love between Indians and included moral instruction. But the essence of his teachings was mystical and centered on visions of the resurrection of the dead and the destruction of the whites.

During the Ghost Dance ceremonies, fatigue and heat induced trances in which dancers saw and conversed with appari-

toward some of the women. It is also possible that the utter humiliation and despair felt by the Sioux prompted them to fire first in what was certainly a suicide attack. The leader of the tribe, Chief Big Foot, suffering from pneumonia at the time of the massacre, would have been unlikely to engage the cavalry troops in so uneven a battle. And many of the Sioux weapons were, it was later determined, missing essential parts and thus useless. Twenty-five soldiers were killed and another thirty-nine were wounded in the melee, but most by "friendly fire" from the Hotchkiss guns (with which the soldiers were not yet entirely familiar) or in hand-to-hand combat. Approximately one hundred and fifty Sioux were killed on the spot, including Big Foot and about fifty women and children. The total number of Indian casualties, including those who died a day or two later (some from exposure to the bitter cold), was three hundred.

The massacre at Wounded Knee marked not only the end of the Indian Wars and the Ghost Dance religion but of Indian civilization on the North American continent. Wovoka once again became Jack Wilson and lived in Nevada, where he died in 1932. The descendants of the original tribes eked out a living on the reservations and were slowly assimilated into American culture to one degree or another. But in 1973, the American Indian Movement (AIM), an organization dedicated to the revitalization of Indian culture and values, made Wounded Knee its rallying cry and drew national attention to its cause by seizing the nearly desolate village.

Contemporary depictions of the Battle of Wounded Knee Creek show the cavalry beleaguered by a large Indian force, when in fact the exact opposite was the case.

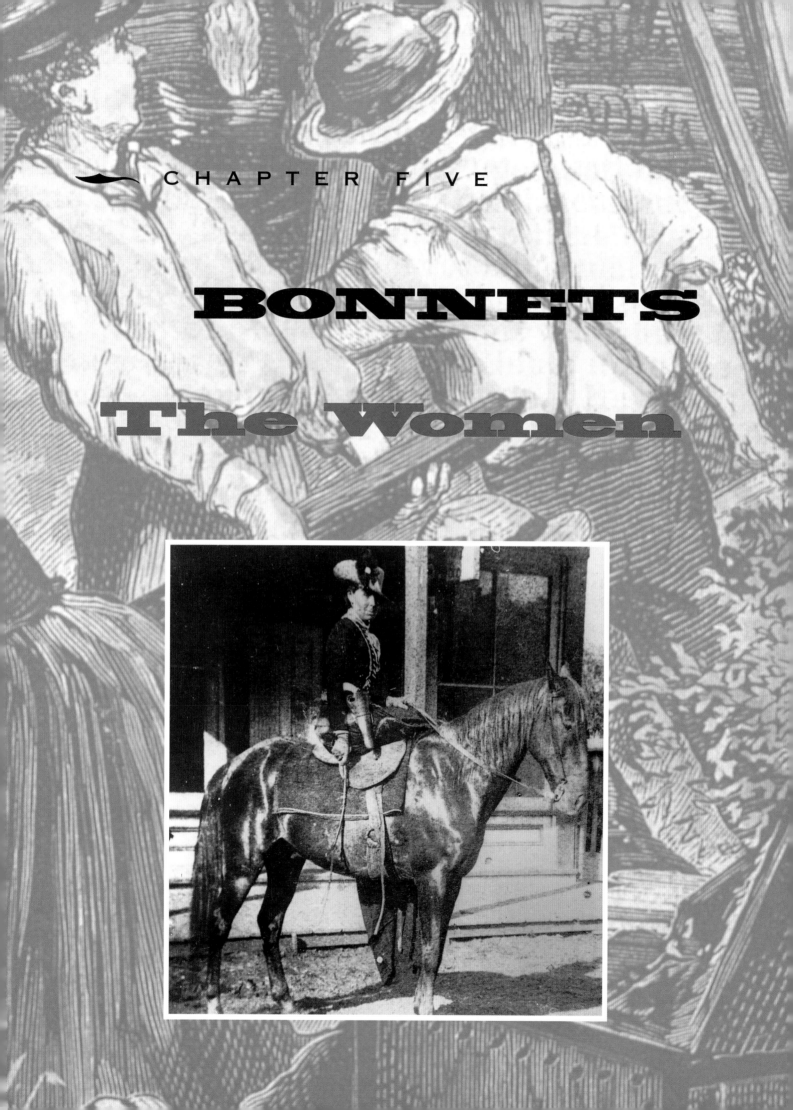

CHAPTER FIVE

BONNETS
The Women

We have already encountered many women in the history of the West, and devoting a special chapter to the women of the West might be considered patronizing if it suggested that the sum total of women's experience in the West was contained in this chapter. The fact is that the large majority of settlers who came West came as families. Each family had to be a self-contained unit capable of providing every service or skill for itself. Most of the skills for which men were trained—agriculture, hunting, warding off attackers—would not be used until the family was settled, so the women were vital to carrying the settlers through the transition period.

Life for women on the frontier was very difficult, and many women, faced with the sudden death or the disappearance of a husband, ended their own lives rather than be enslaved by Indians or other settlers. Establishing a home was very hard work, and some women, hoping to create a home that approximated some idyllic image they had been sold (possibly as part of the effort to get them to leave in the first place), found the squalor and loneliness more than they could bear. Some managed to find their way back east, and others were driven to the only line of work left open to them on the frontier: prostitution.

The prostitutes are often depicted as living charmed and pampered lives, but they had it no easier than their "respectable" sisters. They were usually deeply in debt to a madam or pimp, were subjected to disease and violence from their customers, and often drank themselves to death or committed suicide in some other way. One estimate places more than fifty thousand prostitutes at work in the western territories in the latter half of the nineteenth century, and the poorhouses were filled with women who had been beaten down and dispirited by the profession.

Women were certainly in demand in the West as wives and companions. An informal census of San Francisco in 1849 showed there to be twenty-five hundred women and more than sixty thousand men there. The urban areas quickly filled with failed farmers and miners, and these towns became more hospitable toward women than the prairie, even if the menfolk in them were only marginally civilized. In fact, the primary civilizing influence in towns throughout the West during the period of settlement in the latter half of the nineteenth century were women. They established schools, churches, medical facilities, commerce, and even banks and law enforcement groups. The active role women took in forging a livable society in the West is apparent when one considers the success of two movements

Whiskey and alcoholism were obstacles to the creation of anything resembling a civilized society in the West, and women were at the forefront of the temperance movement throughout the nineteenth century, as is clear from this Currier & Ives poster.

A DRINKING "BEE" AT WHITECHAPEL, DAWSON.

that, though they may have begun in the East, played an even more decisive society-shaping role in the West: the temperance and suffrage movements.

In modern society, it is easy to forget the tide against which both of these movements swam. Opposition came from both men and women, and powerful social, political, business, and even religious forces opposed the two goals. Yet women received the vote in Wyoming and Montana before the passage of the Nineteenth Amendment, and the temperance movement took hold in the Midwest as nowhere else. Followers regarded prohibition in the West to be essential if the unsavory business interests of gambling and prostitution were to be eliminated. It is doubtful whether Carry

Above: Women were not immune to the attractions of drink as a refuge from the dreariness and loneliness of life on the frontier. Here, women gather for a "drinking bee." Left: The Sears, Roebuck catalog gave pioneers the ability to shop for every convenience and was a pivotal supplier of tools, materials, and other supplies on the frontier right into the twentieth century.

The political power of women became clear in the suffrage movement in Wyoming (here depicted in 1888), a state that led the nation in extending the right to vote to women.

Nation's "hetchtations" would have been tolerated had she not had an army of determined women behind her.

Women soon found themselves in the familiar historical position of running a ranch or a business after the death of their husbands—and a number of them, such as Mary Ann Goodnight, became well known for being talented and astute businesspeople. Women found a congenial setting for their talents on the ranch. They were often much more capable of handling animals than were men and more inclined to maintain a ranch and keep it from deteriorating into a heap of rubbish. The ability to make the most of limited provisions was something women had been trained in back east, and it became an essential and valuable skill on the range. When Wild West shows became a popular entertainment across the country and in Europe, there was a large bank of talented women riders and cowgirls from which to choose. Annie Oakley may have been the best and most celebrated, but she was not by a long shot the only female rodeo artist.

Women created an important link between the West and the eastern United States, because they depended on merchants to bring clothing and household items from the East before an indigenous industry base was established. The appearance in the late 1800s of mail-order catalogs from Montgomery Ward and Sears, Roebuck was an important boon to life in the West. These were the largest catalogs, but they were by no means the first. The hunger in the West for items from the East was nearly insatiable, and many catalogs appeared, made their contributions to frontier life, and then quickly disappeared during the late nineteenth century.

And then there were the women who rejected the status quo and decided to impersonate men. Calamity Jane and Laura Bullion (sometime girlfriend of Wild Bunch outlaw Ben Kilpatrick) often dressed as men. And several individuals of note lived for years as men before it was discovered that they were women: Bill Newcomb, a hero of the Mexican War, was in reality Elizabeth Smith; Civil War notable Albert Cashier was in truth Jennie Hodges; and the famous stagecoach driver Charlie Parkhurst kept "his" true identity as a woman hidden until after his death (when a doctor discovered that Charlie must have given birth to a child at some point).

The portrayal of women in the West is (as is clearly the case in almost every other category examined) ludicrous and woefully inadequate, to put it mildly. The best one can say is that authors and filmmakers had no idea of how to place women in their own fantasies of the West and so generally left them out entirely. Partly in response to the Hays Office, which restricted sexual themes in movies, and partly because of the adolescent fantasy world depicted in most westerns—especially B-westerns—women did not appear in many films. When they did appear, they were usually only a vehicle for presenting a danger against which the hero could fight.

Serious female characters, as in the film *High Noon* and in the television series *Gunsmoke*, were sanitized, not for reasons of censorship, but because both directors and audiences did not know what to make of a legitimate woman in an Old West setting. Two notable exceptions stand out so starkly that they are "the exceptions that prove the rule." These are the portrayal of Etta Place by Katherine Ross in the film *Butch Cassidy and the Sundance Kid* and the fictional character Constance Miller, the British madam on the frontier, in the 1971 Robert Altman classic, *McCabe and Mrs. Miller*, based on the Edmund Naughton novel. In both instances—to comic effect in the former and to dramatic in the latter—the women depicted are genuine and individual characters, living lives that bear some relationship to the realities of life in the West.

CALAMITY JANE

Probably the most famous woman of the Old West was Martha Jane Canary (sometimes spelled Cannary), who was known as Calamity Jane. There are all sorts of fanciful stories about how she got her colorful name, just as there are many tales and details of Calamity Jane's life that have become part of the lore of the Old West. It is nearly impossible to say for certain what is true, what is exaggeration, and what is bare-faced lie. Calamity Jane spread so many of these stories herself and peddled them—in barroom tales and in her

Autobiography—wherever she went that no doubt the truth bears only a minor resemblance to the stories.

It is believed that she was born on May 1, 1852, in Missouri, one of many children brought up by Robert and Charlotte Canary on their two-hundred-acre farm. For some unknown reason, the family pulled up stakes in 1863 and set out for Utah. Here is where the first detour from fact occurs, for the legend has it that Jane's parents died

Calamity Jane posing with a rifle at the turn of the century.

en route, and she and her siblings had to be parceled out to various Utah families—which gave rise to one reason she was called Calamity (her calamitous early life in the West). Better evidence indicates that the family arrived intact in the gold-rush town of Virginia City, Montana, and it was here that Jane's parents died. She worked as a dishwasher, nurse, cook, and ox-team driver, becoming adept at the skills of fighting, shooting, and bluffing an opponent. As a young girl without parents, she probably had to defend her honor on a number of occasions.

By the time she was eighteen, Jane had grown to be a tall, muscular woman ("big-boned" was the term often used to describe her) who wore buckskin men's clothing,

carried firearms, and enjoyed the decidedly masculine pleasures of smoking cigars, drinking hard liquor, and cussing. She very likely spent some time as a muleskinner, and these were common occupational pastimes of that trade. She also showed great skill in riding and shooting, and she usually enjoyed the company of men, certainly when they were in the process of getting drunk in the local saloon. Of all the reasons given for her nickname, the one that seems most plausible is that, as she staggered through the saloons and streets too drunk to see or shoot straight, people would say, "Here comes calamity!"

At about this time, she met James Butler "Wild Bill" Hickok in Abilene, Kansas, and then became entangled in his life when she settled in Deadwood, South Dakota. Whether or not the two were legally married has been a matter of dispute for years. The U.S. government recognized this marriage in 1941 when it granted old-age relief to a woman who claimed to be Jean Hickok, daughter of James B. and Martha J. Hickok. She even produced a diary supposedly kept by Calamity Jane, but the government was notoriously lax in checking these matters. Whether or not they were legally married, Wild Bill and Calamity Jane were "an item" and were probably lovers (although one would not have thought the manly Calamity to be Wild Bill's type), and the child that Calamity Jane gave up for adoption in 1873 was probably the pair's love child.

In 1875 Jane attempted to enlist as a soldier in General Crook's cavalry but was drummed out the first time she bathed with the other soldiers. Jane herself told this story, but all photographs of her make it difficult to believe she could be mistaken for a man, however she might disguise herself. She also promoted the legend that she captured the man who shot Wild Bill Hickok in the back in August 1876 (offering a picturesque image of cornering Jack McCall in the Deadwood butcher shop). No evidence exists of Jane's having any involvement in apprehending the killer. She certainly spent

Calamity Jane in Denver with Jack Crawford (right) and an unidentified man. Calamity Jane was the most celebrated of the women of the West who could ride and shoot at least as well as a man, but there were many others whose names and stories have been lost.

some time during that period as part of the Walter Jenney survey expedition to the Black Hills, which gave her a deep knowledge of the area and made her a valuable guide. She lived and worked with a series of prospectors during the gold-rush days in the Black Hills from 1876 to 1880, taking time off in the Deadwood saloons for a raucous bender every now and then.

Jane was briefly married to a Texan named Clinton Burke, a wagon driver in the Black Hills. And though she never waned in her devotion to Hickok—or wavered in her insistence that they had been married—it is by her will that the name "Mrs. M.E. Burke" appears on her tombstone under the larger "Calamity Jane" in the Deadwood cemetery.

From about 1893, Calamity Jane's life followed a regular pattern: she would become a performer in a Wild West show or at a large fair or exposition, only to be fired when her drinking made her unruly and dangerous. She joined the Buffalo Bill Wild West Show in 1893 and toured England with the show, but she was fired for her excessive drinking. The same thing happened in 1896 when she was touring with the Palace Museum Show and again in 1901 when she appeared at the Buffalo Pan-American Exposition. Jane was clearly an alcoholic, and the last years of her life were spent in a pitiful attempt to convince the world she had been the great love of Wild Bill Hickok's life. A photograph of her at Wild Bill's grave was taken in 1903, and she circulated this likeness widely along with tattered copies of her thin autobiography, which she sold for a few cents.

By the summer of 1903, Jane's health had finally been wrecked by the years of hard living and even harder drinking. She was quoted as crying out to the world, "Leave me alone and let me go to hell my own route." The people of Deadwood felt sorry for her and raised some money that would have provided her (and her seven-year-old daughter, of uncertain parentage, then living in a convent) with a small measure of comfort and security. She took the money and drank it up in a binge to end all binges. She spent her last days in poverty, sick with pneumonia, in a dark hotel room in a town near Deadwood. With almost her last breath, she asked that she be buried next to Wild Bill Hickok. She died on August 3, 1903 (a day later than the date on her precarved tombstone), and the people of Deadwood heaved a sigh and buried her near—but not right alongside—the grave of Wild Bill Hickok.

Several excellent biographies of Calamity Jane have appeared over the years, some heightening the mystery surrounding her life. These include J. Leonard Jennewein's 1965 book, *Calamity Jane of the Western Trails*, and James D. Horan's 1952 work, *Desperate Women*. The various portrayals of Calamity Jane on the screen—from the clunky Yvonne DeCarlo in the absurd 1949 film *Calamity Jane Meets Sam Bass* (they never did) to the feminist Jane Alexander in 1984's *Calamity Jane*—have not scratched the surface of this interesting western character, one of the most famous of the Old West.

CATTLE KATE

Ella "Cattle Kate" Watson was born in 1862, in Canada, according to some sources, or in Kansas, according to others, but there is little dispute that she grew up to be a striking woman who was capable of handling both a rifle and a branding iron. Her early marriage to a man named Maxwell ended quickly, and she was forced to travel across the Nebraska-Colorado-Wyoming plains earning her living as a prostitute. In 1883 she settled in Carbon County, Wyoming, and became the common-law wife of James Averill, a saloon keeper and general-store owner in Sweetwater, a cattle-raising area in Johnson County, Wyoming. The pair had a son, Tom, in 1884, although throughout her years with Jim, Ella never ceased earning a living as a prostitute.

In 1888 Ella and young Tom joined Jim in Sweetwater, and Ella set up a homestead adjacent to Jim's, still offering her services to the local cowhands. Averill staked Ella to a home and corrals, and soon the cattle on Ella's land began to multiply, as cowboys paid Ella in cows sneaked off their ranches when they had no money. The local ranchers considered this pilferage part of "the price of doing business," and Ella was given the lighthearted name "Cattle Kate." The fact was, once Ella let it be known that she would accept payment in cattle, the foremen of the ranches paid many of their cowboys with cattle—a cheaper means of payment—so that quite a few of the cows on Ella's spread bore the altered brands of the large ranches.

Averill spearheaded the homestead movement, which was organized by the small ranchers who resisted the efforts of the cattlemen—the absentee landlords of the large spreads capitalized by eastern money—to impose prices and shipping policy on them. Averill's main target was Albert J. Bothwell, a wealthy cattleman whose spread bordered nearly everyone's in the county. A killing winter in 1887 had nearly wiped out the homesteaders, and Bothwell's private war against the "nesters," the name given the ranchers who had lost their herds and land in the frost and who set up makeshift farms and ranches

in an effort to try again, was cruel and relentless. Bothwell and the other members of the Wyoming Stock Growers' Association hired private guards and vigilantes (called "regulators"), who snatched whole families from their homes, accused them of cattle rustling, and lynched them. Averill organized the local ranchers, but their resources were limited, so he turned to the only other tool at his disposal: the press. He wrote a series of scathing letters to the local paper accusing Bothwell of being responsible for every foul deed committed by the regulators. The letters unleashed a fury on the part of the homesteaders that made it impossible for the cattlemen to turn to the local courts to punish anyone who stole their cattle or attacked their ranch hands.

The real "Cattle Kate," Ella Watson.

A scene from the film Heaven's Gate *showing Isabelle Huppert, playing a character inspired by Ella Watson, dancing with Kris Kristofferson.*

Knowing the relationship between Watson and Averill, and knowing that much of the cattle on the Watson spread could be shown to have altered brands (some because they were legitimate payment, some because cowhands had helped themselves to a cow), Bothwell accused Watson of being a cattle rustler and demanded action from the authorities. When none was forthcoming—mainly because local sentiment was strongly in favor of Ella and Averill—the regulators stormed Ella's home when Jim was there, dragged the pair out of the cabin, and lynched them. The incident touched off what became known as the Johnson County War of 1892, the largest confrontation between large landowners and small homesteaders in the West.

The cattlemen hired a veritable army, composed mainly of Texans, to fight the homesteaders for them. Led by Major Frank Wolcott, these hired gunmen (sometimes known as the "Invaders") scored some early victories, but news of their activities soon reached the county seat, Buffalo. A throng of three hundred new settlers soon appeared on the scene, and, led by Johnson County sheriff Red Angus, they besieged the cattlemen's army at the TA Ranch. Only the intervention of the Sixth Cavalry stationed in Fort McKinney saved the Invaders, and although they were taken prisoner and expected to stand trial for their actions, beginning with the lynching of Ella Watson and James Averill, the political influence of the wealthy cattlemen prevented a trial from ever taking place.

The impact of the Johnson County War was far-reaching and long lasting. The hiring of the Invaders created a rift between the poorer people of the area and the wealthy landowners that has been a factor in Wyoming politics for a century. The incident also created a tension between the northern states of Wyoming and Montana, on the one hand, and Texas and Oklahoma, where most of the Invaders hailed from, on the other. The only hero of the war was Nathan Champion, a friend and supporter of Averill who held off a siege of a band of Invaders on the KC Ranch.

The Johnson County War was also the subject of one of the most disastrous films in the history of filmmaking, *Heaven's Gate*. The 1980 film became famous for costing thirty-six million dollars and being seen by virtually no one because it was panned by the critics. The story only just barely follows the history of the Johnson County War—perhaps Isabelle Huppert is supposed to be Ella Watson, but the facts surrounding her life as presented on the screen are not close to the life Ella led—and the film was criticized for being (of all things) out of focus. The debacle turned the movie into a cliché and a synonym for an expensive bomb capable of driving a studio into bankruptcy, which is exactly what *Heaven's Gate* did to United Artists.

BELLE STARR

The career of Belle Starr is one of the most celebrated in all the West, complete with moral elements and tantalizing mysteries. Her biographers are quick to point out that Starr was not a pretty woman, and they direct the reader's attention to photographs. Some believe she benefited from the sparsenes of the female population of the West, but she often established liaisons with men who were celebrated (if only as outlaws) in their time. There was no doubt that Belle Starr

was a romantic with what might be described as a liberal attitude toward sex.

She was born Myra Belle Shirley in Arkansas (not Missouri, as she later claimed) on February 5, 1848, to a wealthy family who moved to Carthage, Missouri, when Belle was an infant. Her father, John Shirley, established a successful hotel business in Carthage, and Myra Belle was educated at the Carthage Female Academy, a finishing school where she learned languages and piano. The Civil War profoundly disrupted the Shirley family: the eldest son, Edward, was killed and the Shirley Hotel was burned to the ground. The family salvaged what it could from the ruins and left the area for Texas, settling in 1863 in Scyne, a small town east of Dallas. John Shirley once again proved his business acumen and in a few years built another thriving hotel business.

In Scyne, Starr met Cole Younger, one of Quantrill's Raiders, who hid out at the

The notorious Belle Starr riding in a refined sidesaddle style, probably just for this portrait.

A wanted poster with Belle Starr's maiden name.

Shirley place in between raids. She and Younger became lovers, and Younger may have been the father of Starr's first child, a daughter whom she named Pearl. About the same time—1866—Starr was being courted by a childhood sweetheart named Jim Reed, with whom she had had a romance back in Carthage. Reed, who had been a member of the outlaw gang led by Tom Starr, asked Belle's father for her hand in marriage, but the elder Shirley was not pleased with the prospect of having an avowed criminal for a son-in-law. He changed his mind when it became clear that Belle was once again "with child" (though it was not certain to anyone whether the father was Reed or Younger), and the pair were married. Belle gave birth to a son, Edward. She coddled Pearl and abused Edward their entire lives, supporting the notion that one was a child of the beloved Younger and the other was the child of the despised Reed.

The Reed family spent a short period in California, staying just long enough to determine that the authorities were sufficiently well equipped to deal with train robbers and horse thieves, and by 1869 they were back in Dallas. It was during this period that Belle gained her reputation as a "bandit queen" as she rode alongside her husband on his robberies, riding her famous mare, Venus, and wearing velvet riding skirts and feather-topped hats. Amazingly, she was never positively identified or arrested, though her reputation spread far and wide.

Predictably, Reed was killed in 1874 by a deputy sheriff. Belle left her children with her parents and moved to Dallas, dealing cards and shooting up the saloons. It was also in this period that she met Jesse James. A photograph of Belle with a man identified as Blue Duck has led biographers to believe that she had become involved with an Indian, but others believe the name to be an alias, and the relationship not to have been very serious. When things became too hot in Dallas, she moved to Galena, Kansas, where she lived with Bruce Younger, a cousin of Cole's. Then she moved to Oklahoma and set up her own horse-stealing and cattle-rustling operation as the wife of Tom Starr's son, Sam. The torch she carried for Younger (Cole or Bruce) must have burned hotly, because she called her spread "Younger's Bend."

Belle and Sam carried on a thriving horse-stealing business, at one point drawing the attention of the U.S. marshal, who offered a ten-thousand-dollar reward for their capture. They were finally arrested and brought before the "Hanging Judge," Isaac Parker, who gave the pair surprisingly light sentences of six months. Returning from prison in the fall of 1883, Belle lost interest in Sam and took up once again with Blue Duck. When he disappeared from the scene in 1886, she carried on a torrid affair with John Middleton, a man wanted for the murder of a sheriff. It seems Belle was planning to run away with Middleton, but he

Belle Starr and a man who has often (but not definitively) been identified as her husband, Blue Duck.

was found one day with his head literally blown off by a shotgun blast, probably at Sam's hand. Sam himself was shot dead in December 1886 during a barroom brawl.

Belle's next husband was Jim July, a nephew of Tom Starr. On February 2, 1889, Belle accompanied Jim part of the way to Fort Smith, having convinced him to stand trial for a series of offenses. She promised she would obtain the best legal counsel available to get him off. She let July continue on alone and headed back to Younger's Bend. Before she got there, someone shot her in the back with a shotgun. Many theories were advanced about who the culprit was. Some believed July had doubled back,

Right: Annie Oakley became famous all over North America and Europe for her incomparable equestrian and shooting skills. Opposite: In one of her most famous and astonishing tricks, Oakley demonstrates the technique of over-the-shoulder shooting.

done the deed, and then continued on to Fort Smith—and that he killed her because she was heading, not for a lawyer, but toward a rendezvous with yet another lover. Attention also focused on her son, Ed, who had been whipped by his mother only that morning. July accused a tenant who had quarreled with Belle and whom she had threatened to turn in to authorities in Florida, where he was wanted. No evidence could be found implicating the tenant, Watson; he was killed by a posse that finally caught up with him in 1910. No one was charged with the murder, and the identity of the killer became a famous mystery of the Old West. There was even a woman who, in 1971, came forward with the unlikely story that her grandmother admitted to her on her death bed that it had been she who had killed Belle Starr, mistakenly believing her to be a neighbor she thought was carrying on with her husband.

ANNIE OAKLEY

There are at least two "Annie Oakleys," and it has not always been easy for historians and biographers to tie all of them together into one person. Annie Oakley was born Phoebe Ann Moses in rural Ohio on August 13, 1860 (or possibly 1864). Her father died when she was four years old, and she was placed, along with her seven siblings, with foster parents. She was abused by her foster family and ran away in search of her mother (who, as it turned out, was looking for her). By the age of twelve, she was already proving her prowess with a rifle, supplying a Cincinnati hotel with quail and game. In 1875 the hotel owner, Charlie Katzenberger, arranged for

Phoebe to enter a shooting contest against sharpshooter Frank Butler, who was performing in a touring show at the Coliseum Theater. Phoebe outshot Butler and relieved him of the hundred-dollar prize.

Butler got wind of a plan Katzenberger was concocting to have Phoebe follow the sharpshooter from town to town and capture the prize at each stop, so he offered to make the youngster part of the show. She assumed the stage name Annie Oakley (after the Cincinnati neighborhood in which the hotel was located) and became a sensation wherever she performed. In time,

In her later years (this photo is from 1922) Oakley was still famous and still giving shooting lessons.

Butler realized that everyone was coming to see Annie and not him, so he stopped performing and became her manager. In 1880 Butler and Annie were married.

At one stop on their tour in New Orleans, Annie auditioned for a show that was near bankruptcy at the time but that had a wider reputation than Butler's: Buffalo Bill's Rocky Mountain and Prairie Exhibition. Annie performed for Buffalo Bill Cody in the pouring rain, and the old showman knew instantly that he had a blockbuster talent on his hands. He reorganized the entire show as Buffalo Bill's Wild West

Show, and it became an immediate success. Annie toured (with Frank) in the show for seventeen years as the star attraction. She added trick riding to her repertoire and performed many feats of sharpshooting that seasoned professionals found stunning. Among her most famous were shooting a dime out of her husband's fingers and a cigarette out of his mouth, slicing a playing card held sideways in the air, hitting all five spades on a five-of-spades with five shots, and hitting everything from coins to glass balls tossed in the air—any number at a time. Her signature trick of shooting holes in a playing card gave rise to the slang American term for a complimentary ticket to an entertainment event, called an Annie Oakley to this day. (Managers would punch complimentary tickets with a punch many times so that they couldn't be resold.) She perfected the art of shooting backward over her shoulder while aiming with a mirror, and she exhibited incredible sharpshooting skills while riding a horse.

Annie was a sensation when Buffalo Bill's show toured Europe. Sitting Bull was part of the show in 1885 and was no less amazed than everyone else with Annie's abilities. He gave her the name "Little Miss Sure Shot," a name that stayed with her throughout her career. The Crown Prince Wilhelm of Germany (later to become Kaiser Wilhelm II) insisted that she shoot a cigarette out of his mouth, and, when she was challenged by Grand Duke Michael of Russia to a shooting contest, she refused Buffalo Bill's request that she throw the contest. Her victory made her an international celebrity.

Butler managed his wife's career very well, though her skill never waned through her professional life. At one point, Annie changed her legal last name for some reason from "Moses" to "Mozee." Her personal life was puritanical and sedate in the extreme; she spent time between shows engaged in her two favorite pastimes: knitting and embroidery. She was nothing like the rambunctious hellion of Irving Berlin's classic musical, *Annie Get Your Gun*, or the strong-willed character portrayed by Barbara Stanwyck in George Stevens's 1935 film, *Annie Oaklie*.

In October 1901 the train carrying Buffalo Bill's Wild West Show collided head-on with a freight train near Lexington, Kentucky. Few people were hurt in the crash, but Annie was seriously injured and spent several months in the hospital, undergoing five life-saving operations. After two years of determined effort, Annie not only was able to walk (she had been paralyzed after the crash), but also had regained her shooting ability. A spring was absent from her step and her hair had become white, but her eye was as good as ever and she returned to performing.

After the era of the Wild West shows was over, Annie was still in demand. She performed in several stage plays about the West and even toured army bases during World War I instructing soldiers on shooting techniques. In 1921 Annie and Frank were in an automobile accident; Frank walked away, but Annie never walked or fired a rifle again. She spent her last years in Ohio and died on November 3, 1926. Frank died twenty days later.

Most of the early information about Annie Oakley's life came from a work written by Courtney Cooper, a publicist for her various shows. As one might expect, the Cooper work sometimes accepted publicity as fact. Annie's niece, Annie Swartwount, published a more accurate account in 1947, and the definitive account, by Walter Havighurst, was published as *Annie Oakley of the Wild West* in 1954.

The most popular image of Annie Oakley was provided by the television show that

Temperance crusader Carry Nation with her signature hatchet.

starred Gail Davis in the title role. Davis was discovered by Gene Autry at a rodeo where she was performing many stunts reminiscent of the feats Annie used to perform. The show, which ran from 1953 to 1956, was one of the most popular children's programs of the 1950s.

CARRY NATION

Carry Nation's career as a champion of temperance bears so many interesting parallels to modern activism and has such a modern flavor that it is no wonder that she has become an inspiration for activists in the latter half of this century. Whiskey (and alcohol in general) was so central a part of western life that many people on both sides of the prohibition issue (and on both sides of the issue of Nation's sanity) paid careful attention to her fortunes as a temperance radical.

She was born Carry Amelia Moore in Kentucky in 1846 to a family that moved often and found itself perpetually on the brink of bankruptcy. It seems her mother was deeply psychotic and her father a business failure, and both factors contributed to forging an independent spirit in young Carry. In 1867 she married Civil War veteran and Union physician Charles Gloyd, who was an alcoholic. Gloyd died while Carry

Above: Though the hatchets were primarily symbolic, they were always capable of doing real damage to saloons and whiskey barrels—and frequently did. Right: This nineteenth-century cartoon of Carry Nation (her first name misspelled on the placard) captures her determined yet whimsical nature. In spite of the fact that official temperance movements shunned her, Nation's crusade kept the prohibition issue at the forefront of America's consciousness.

was expecting, and a daughter was born. Carry eked out a living for herself and her daughter by teaching school—in spite of her family's poverty and all of the moving, she had received a good education. She left teaching in 1877, when she married David Nation, a minister nineteen years her senior. In the late 1880s, the Nations settled in Medicine Lodge, Kansas, where David was a church minister, and Carry volunteered with the local temperance society.

In 1900 Carry became frustrated by the ineffectiveness of a decade-long effort to close the saloons of Medicine Lodge, so she tried a new tactic. Claiming she was being driven by "visions," she energized the other temperance volunteers and launched a series of attacks on the saloons. A tall and imposing woman, Nation was able to convince others to join her in destroying the saloons with small hatchets that became emblematic of the temperance movement. She toured many towns in Kansas, leading marches on the local saloons. Kansas was, at the time, a "dry state," having already passed laws prohibiting liquor, but the laws were rarely enforced. Nation was able to confuse the authorities by claiming her hatchet-wielding mobs were only carrying out the law. On only a few occasions were fines levied against her, and they were nearly always paid by the supporters of her cause. Although she did not found the Women's Christian Temperance Union—the WCTU—her activities breathed new life into the organization and gave new impetus to the prohibition movement.

In 1901 she divorced her husband and toured the Midwest, lecturing and promoting her activist point of view. After a decade of rabble-rousing (and selling quite a few souvenir hatchets at meetings and lectures), Nation's energy was spent, and she retired to Arkansas where she wrote a well-received autobiography, *The Use and Need for the Life of Carry A. Nation.* By the time Prohibition was made a part of the constitution, Carry Nation had been all but forgotten. But during the ten years prior to passage of the Twenty-first Amendment, Kansas strictly enforced its antiliquor laws, and that was certainly part of Carry Nation's legacy.

Several gripping biographies have been written about Carry Nation, but filmmakers have not yet discovered this very interesting life, metaphor and fountainhead for many late twentieth-century social phenomena.

POKER ALICE

Poker Alice, late in life, but still scandalous with a cigar clamped firmly in her jaws.

lice Ivers was a bundle of contradictions, but that did not stop her from becoming one of the most famous women of the Old West. She was best known as "Poker Alice," and she proved her poker-playing talents many times in some of the most intensely competitive gambling parlors of the West.

Alice came to America from England sometime before 1870, when she was in her teens. Her father was a schoolteacher in England, and he continued teaching in Colorado, where the family settled. Alice married a miner named Duffield, but a mining accident left her a widow before she was twenty-one. After her husband died, Alice frequented the gambling halls of Colorado out of sheer boredom. She observed and learned, not only the nuances of the game, but also the noncard-playing elements of poker, such as cigar smoking and being able to handle a .45. When gold was discovered in South Dakota,

she moved to Deadwood and became a professional dealer.

At various times, Poker Alice again tried marriage and settled down to farm life, but her husbands never seemed to last and she was soon back at the gaming tables. In 1910 Poker Alice opened her own place—a combination saloon, gambling hall, and brothel—between Fort Meade and the town of Sturgis, South Dakota. It was here that she became nationally known, possibly because it was one of the few establishments in the country that openly flaunted the law and served liquor. Alice's insistence that gambling activities not take place on Sunday and that her establishment be closed on that day was often pointed to as the reason the authorities looked the other way. In all likelihood, a large payroll that included a government official was responsible for the law leaving her alone. Poker Alice's Saloon closed in the late 1920s, and Alice lived in Sturgis till her death in 1930.

Bibliography

The literature of the Old West is vast, and every generation finds itself starting all over, creating a new corpus of work with new perspectives and new insights. No doubt readers will profit from reading classic treatments like Ray Allen Billington's *Westward Expansion* (3rd edition. Indianapolis: Macmillan, 1960), Walter Prescott Webb's *The Great Plains* (Ginn, 1931), or even Bernard De Voto's rousing books on the American frontier. But more modern works will contain not only new information, but a new orientation and appreciation of the place of the West in American history. Here are several that I think will provide any reader with a great introduction to the subject.

Brown, Dee. *Bury My Heart At Wounded Knee: An Indian History of the American West.* Austin, Tex.: Holt, Reinhart and Winston, 1971.

Without exaggeration, one of the great books of the century and a must-read for every American. A great follow-up volume would be Alvin M. Josephy's The Nez Perce Indians and the Opening of the Northwest *(New Haven, Conn.: Yale University Press, 1965).*

Hawgood, John A. *America's Western Frontier.* Knopf, 1967.

A highly readable and balanced view by a British historian. A splendid companion volume would be Alvin M. Josephy's The Indian Heritage of America *(Boston: Houghton Mifflin, 1968).*

Lamar, Howard R., ed. *The Reader's Encyclopedia of the American West.* New York: Crowell, 1977.

Soon to be issued in a second, enlarged edition, this is a work that never ceases to amaze. A livelier albeit briefer and less scholarly work is Denis McLoughlin's Wild and Woolly: An Encyclopedia of the Old West *(New York: Doubleday, 1975).*

Milner, Clyde A., II, Carol A. O'Connor, and Martha A. Sandweiss, eds. *The Oxford History of the American West.* New York: Oxford University Press, 1994.

A large, omnibus volume with a wealth of material, data, and images. As much a tribute to the world of publishing as to the field of Western studies.

Utley, Robert M. *The Lance and the Shield: The Life and Times of Sitting Bull.* New York: Holt, 1993.

A singular work. Of all the many works on Sitting Bull (such as Stanley Vestal's 1957 biography) and Custer (including Evan Hunter's popular classic Son of the Morning Star*), this one is sure to endure, and should be read first and last.*

White, Richard. *It's Your Misfortune and None of My Own: A New History of the American West.* Norman, Okla.: University of Oklahoma Press, 1991.

Slowly but surely being recognized as the most outstanding book about the American West of the last quarter century. Makes generous use of maps from Warren A. Beck and Ynez D. Haase's Historical Atlas of the American West *(Norman, Okla.: University of Oklahoma Press, 1989), a landmark work of its kind.*

Two books that have played a major role in changing traditional views of the American West are:

Athearn, Robert G. *The Mythic West in Twentieth-Century America.* Lawrence, Kans.: University Press of Kansas, 1986.

A wonderful summation of a lifetime of thought and research.

Limerick, Patricia Nelson. *The Legacy of Conquest: The Unbroken Past of the American West.* New York: Norton, 1987.

An excellent example of a more mature understanding of the Old West and its influence on current history.

I have enjoyed and learned much from several books by James D. Horan and by William H. Goetzmann, especially the former's *The Outlaws* (Prinevill, Oreg.: Bonanza, 1968) and the latter's *Exploration and Empire* (New York: Knopf, 1966). Happily, their works remain in print and continue to find an appreciative readership.

Finally, several excellent illustrated works have been issued by Time-Life, Reader's Digest, and the Smithsonian Institution, as well as other publishers. *Trailblazers: The Men and Women Who Forged the West*, by Constance Jones (New York: MetroBooks, 1995), is a fine example of the exciting integration of text and image that this subject permits and encourages. Among the best of this genre, however, remain those issued by American Heritage, including:

Brandon, William. *The American Heritage Book of Indians.* New York: Simon & Schuster, 1961.

Lavender, David. *The American Heritage History of the Great West.* New York: Simon & Schuster, 1965.

Utley, Robert M., and Wilcomb E. Washburn. *The American Heritage History of the Indian Wars.* New york: Simon & Schuster, 1964.

This is considered one of the best titles of the American Heritage series.

Photography Credits

Alaska State Library, Collection: P.E. Larss, Photo: PCA 41–53: p. 173 top

Archive Photos: p. 122

Courtesy, Colorado Historical Society: File 5941: p.126–127; File 44914: p. 164

Corbis-Bettmann Archive: pp. 1, 6–7, 8, 10, 11, 12–13, 17 inset, 18, 21, 22, 23 top & bottom, 24–25, 26 top, 31 top, 32, 34, 38 top & bottom, 39 bottom, 40, 41 top & bottom, 42, 44, 45, 46, 49, 54–55, 55 inset, 56, 58, 59, 60, 61 top, 62, 63, 64, 65, 66, 68, 69, 70, 71, 73, 74, 75, 77, 78, 79, 86, 90, 91, 94 bottom, 96, 97, 98–99, 100–101, 102, 103, 104, 106 top & bottom, 111 top & bottom, 112, 113, 115, 116 top & bottom, 117, 118, 119, 123 top & bottom, 124, 126 inset, 128, 129 bottom, 131, 132, 133, 135, 136, 137 bottom, 142, 146, 147, 148 bottom, 149, 150, 151, 152, 153, 155, 156–157, 158 top & bottom, 159, 160, 161 bottom, 162 top & bottom, 168, 169, 170–171, 171 inset, 172, 174, 175, 176, 180, 181, 182, 183, 188 top & bottom

Denver Public Library, Western History Department: pp. 177, 189

Courtesy of Kansas State Historical Society: p. 37

Kobal Collection: pp. 35, 108

Library of Congress: pp. 2–3, 9, 43, 57, 121, 129 top, 138

Minnesota Historical Society: Artists: Anton Gag, Christian Heller and Alexander Schendinger, 1893: pp. 144–145

Courtesy of the Museum of New Mexico, photo by A. Frank Randall, negative 43061: p. 137 bottom; photo by Edward S. Curtis, negative 65118: p. 148 top

Courtesy of The National Museum of the American Indian/Smithsonian Institution, negative 31502: p. 154

Reuters/Corbis-Bettmann: p. 14

Smithsonian Institution: p. 167

Springer/Corbis-Bettmann: pp. 28 top & bottom, 48, 50

UPI/Corbis-Bettmann: pp. 15, 39 top, 67, 76, 93, 94 top, 107, 184, 185, 186, 187

Western History Collections, University of Oklahoma Library: pp. 19, 20, 26 bottom, 27, 52, 53, 80, 82 top & bottom, 83 top & bottom, 84, 89 all, 109, 134, 139, 140, 141, 143, 161 top

Wyoming Division of Cultural Resources: pp. 16–17, 30, 31 bottom, 33, 179

Index